MINDSCAPES
AN ARTIST'S THOUGHTS AND VISIONS
by Karen Haughey

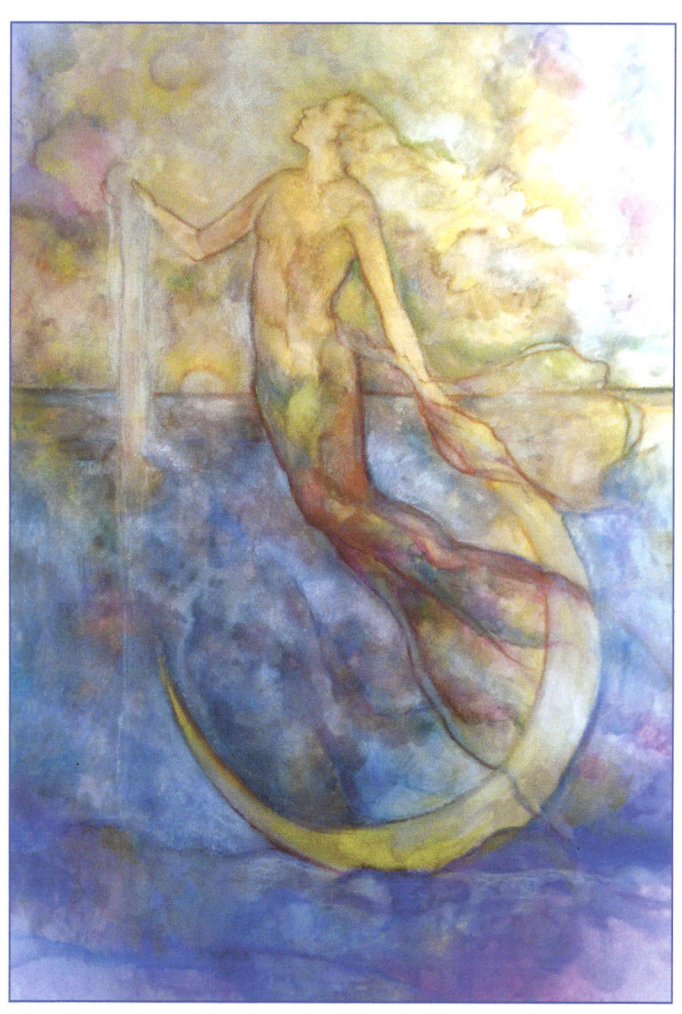

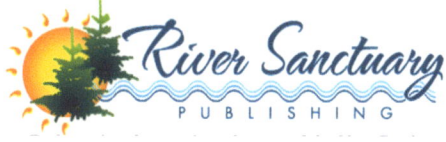

Felton, California

Mindscapes

Copyright ©2019 by Karen Haughey

All rights reserved. No part of this book may be reproduced in any form or by any electronic or mechanical means including information storage and retrieval systems, without permission in writing from the author. The only exception is by reviewer, who may quote short excerpts in a review.

First Edition

ISBN 978-1-935914-91-4

BOOK AND COVER DESIGN BY MELANIE GENDRON
melaniegendron999@gmail.com

COVER AND INTERIOR ART
Karen Haughey

FRONT COVER ART: "Moon Mermaid"

BACK COVER ART: "The Rotation of Light"

Printed in the United States of America

To order additional copies please visit:
www.riversanctuarypublishing.com

River Sanctuary Publishing
P.O. Box 1561
Felton, CA 95018
www.riversanctuarypublishing.com

Dedicated to the awakening of the New Earth

ART IS ONE STEP FROM THE VISIBLY KNOWN TOWARD THE UNKNOWN.
—Kahlil Gibran

MINDSCAPES

AN ARTIST'S THOUGHTS AND VISIONS.

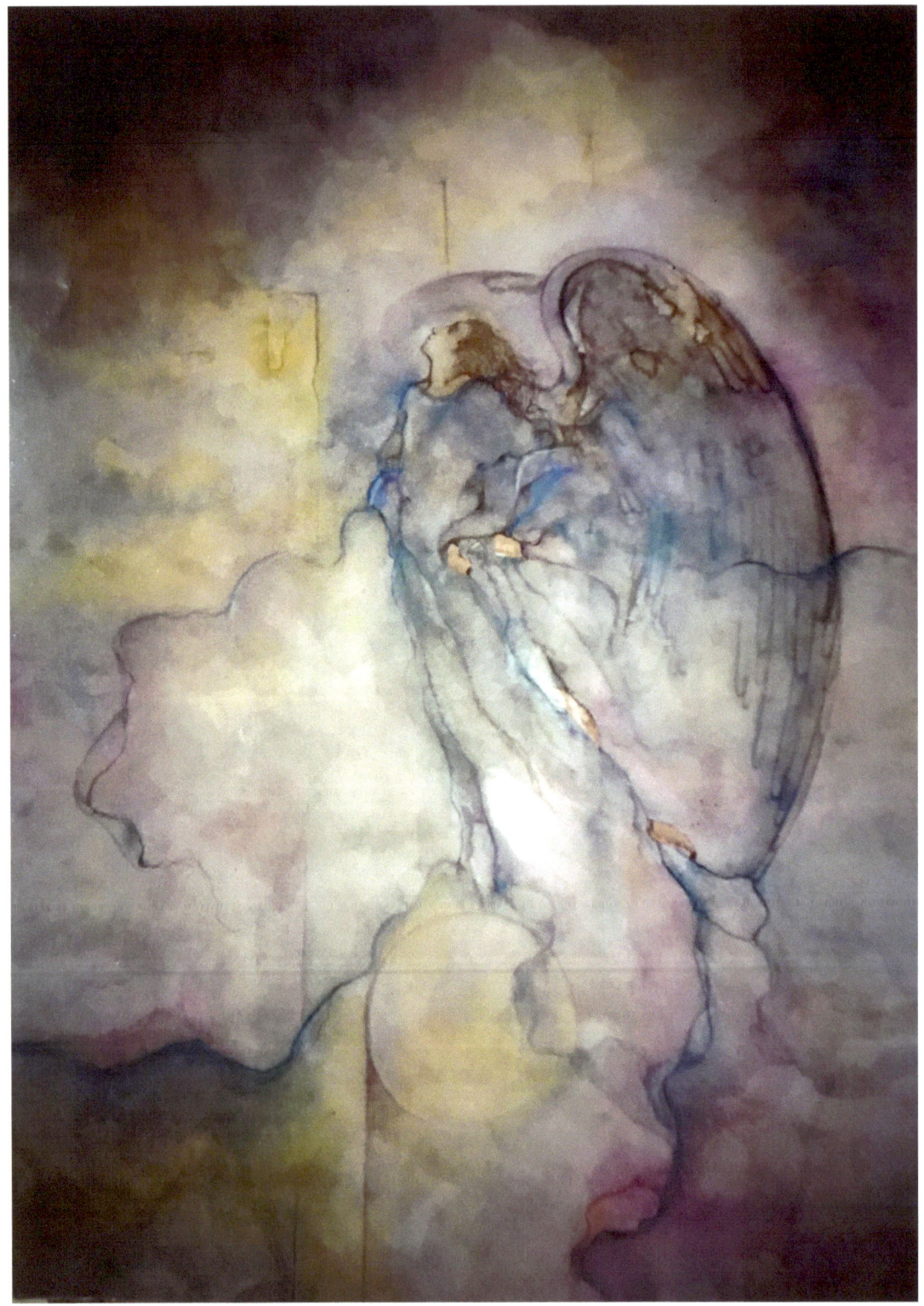

The Ascension of Saint Michael

Karen Haughey created this painting for Unity Church in Fremont, California in 1993, which was also featured in her first book, Angels, Guardians of the Light, published in 1995. It was just recently placed in the historic Saint Michael's Church in Livermore, California where it will remain in their private collection.

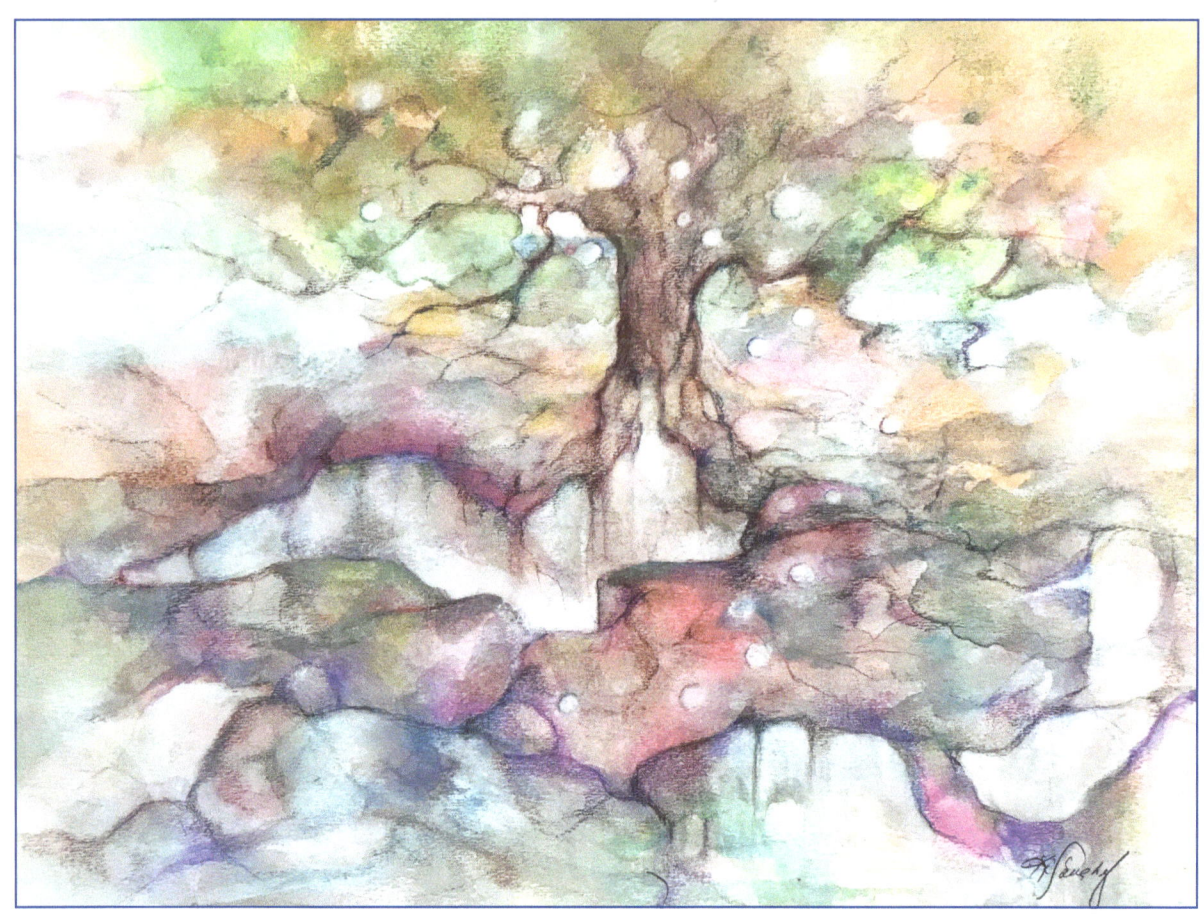

Fairy Bridge

Deep within an unknown forest stands the Fairy Bridge and the fairies mystical tree house.
Mortals may not visit, other than through the creativity of their minds and hearts
Then, if they listen they will hear the flutter of tiny wings, should they be silent.

INTRODUCTION

After my last book, *Angels, Guardians of the Light* was published by Hay House in 1995, my journey continued onward in multifaceted layers that consisted of travel, giving seminars and lectures, and later on being called into the ministry, which transitioned into healthcare chaplaincy. I have continued to serve professionally for the past twenty years in the same capacity.

I did not paint for a period of sixteen years, due to personal circumstances. I eventually was inspired to pick up my brush again several years ago, and haven't stopped painting since. I wasn't confident after so much time had passed, that I would ever paint again, but the dormant seed of creativity sprang forth once again. Afterwards, it felt like I was on an invisible time line with the urge to paint daily. It also carried a familiar energy when I began to paint angelic and ethereal subject matter which was not popular during that time period.

I have been painting most of my life, developing my own style and technique without prompting or expectation around 1984. Many of critics told me I was breaking all the rules by mixing mediums and painting subject matter that was not considered marketable. I have never been one to follow the crowd.

All of the paintings published within this book, *Mindscapes*, have resulted over the past two years.

Thank you so much!

Karen Haughey

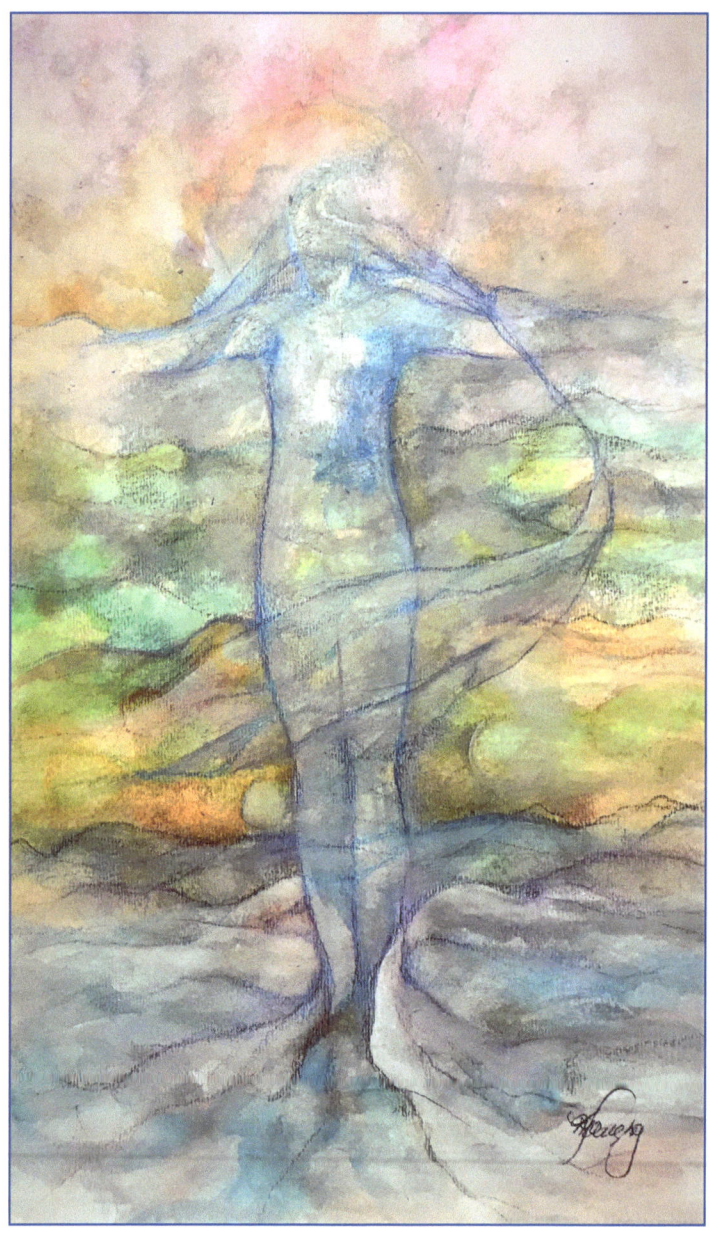

Wind

You cannot see the wind as it moves, but can sense its presence
while it dances through the trees or plays in your hair. You can also experience
its duality and fury while it stirs the waves of the ocean during a storm.
The elements are somewhat like humans.
They can be harmonious, gentle and balanced, or disruptive and wild.

Contents

Title Page Art: Flight 1
The Ascension of Saint Michael 5
Fairy Bridge 6
Introduction 7
Wind 8
Hiding Places 10
Winter and Spring 11
Teaching Peace 12
Seasonal Mosaic 14
A Path Less Traveled 15
City of Hope 16
Vessel 18
Sailing Vessel 19
High Tide 20
Wonderment 21
The Wishing Chair 22
Nature 24
Repose 25
Cat Tales 26
Mindscape 27
Morning Conversation 28
Peaceful Voyage 30
Slumber 31
Hidden Cove 32
Cocoon 34
Windows of the Mind 35
Prism 36
Blessing Tree 37
Drift 38
Profusion Mandala 40
Sunset 42
About the Author 43

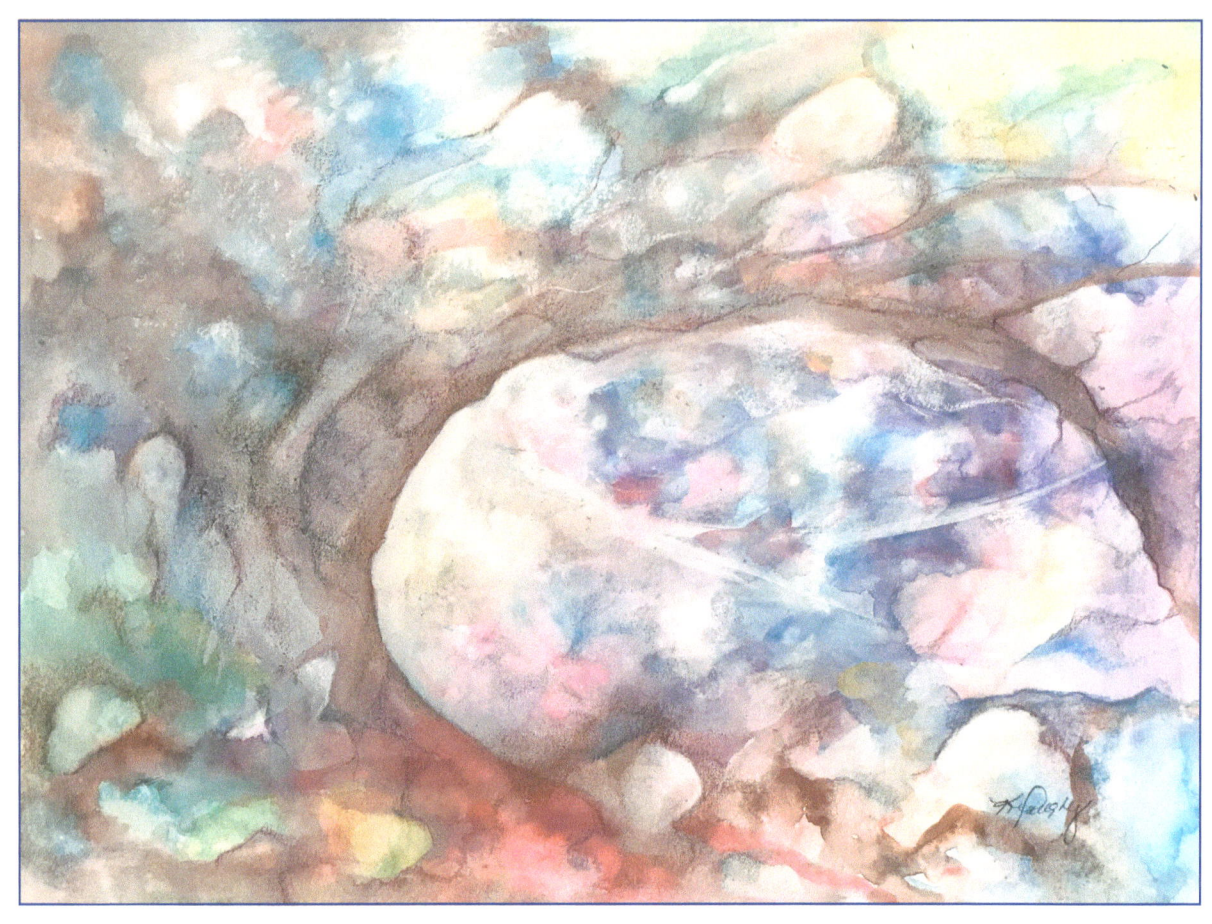

Hiding Places

Allow your imagination to wander through
these peaceful woods and lush wilderness.
What do you see, feel and experience?
You may find many places to hide, or a special place
to rest peacefully along your journey.

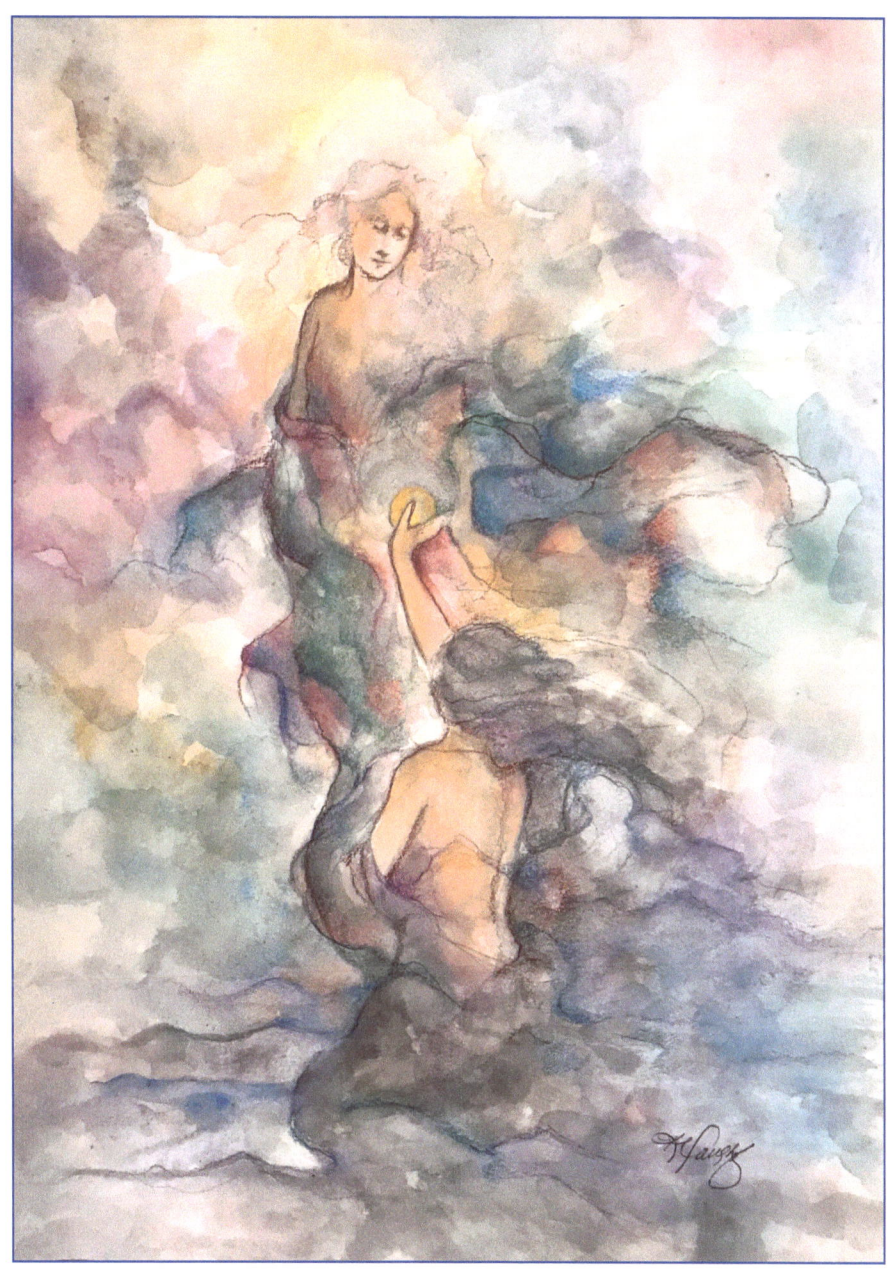

Winter and Spring

During the winter, when all seems dormant, cold and asleep,
there lies a seed of hope that when awakened by spring
becomes the manifestation and renewal
of beauty, hope and warmth.

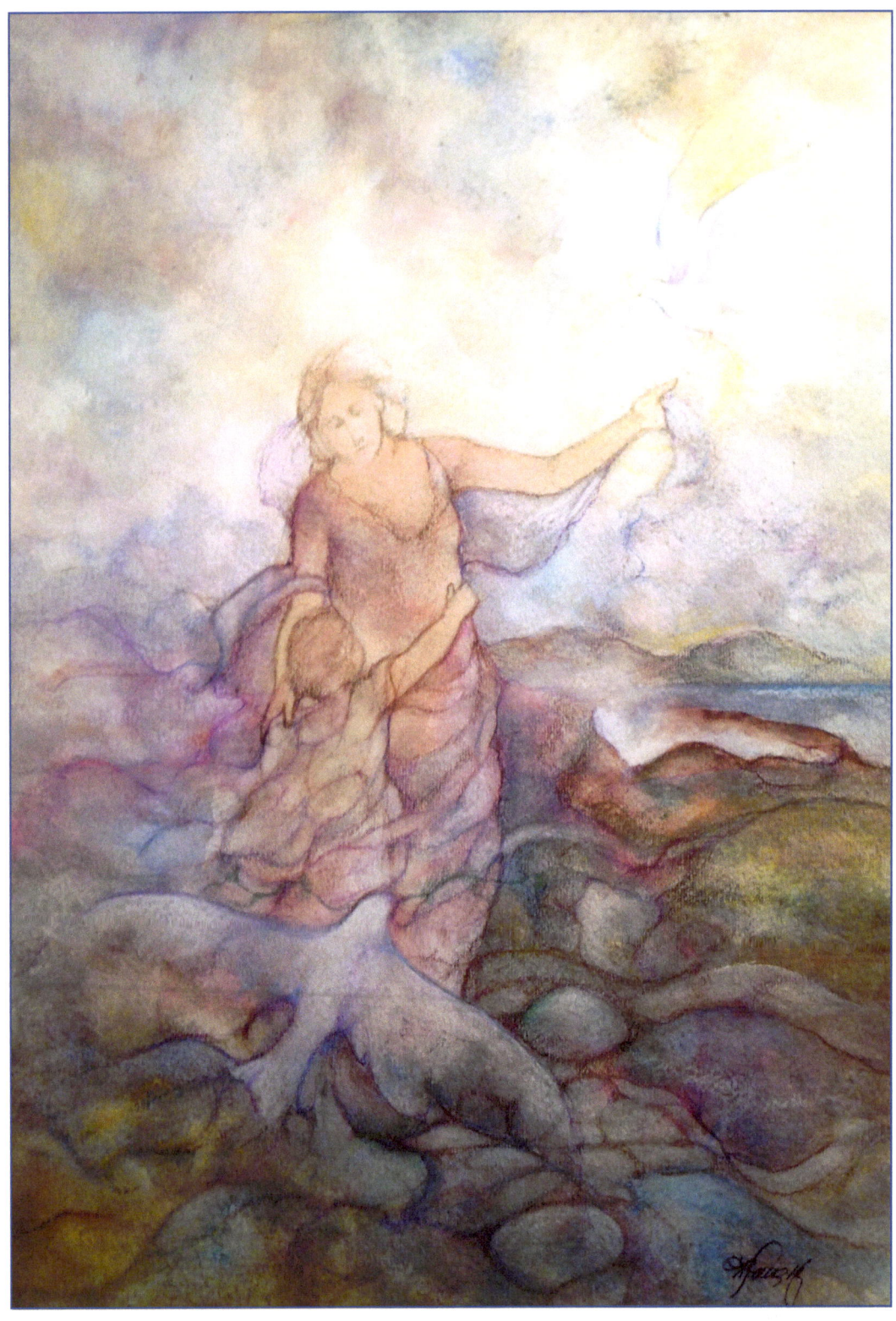

TEACHING PEACE

The Wisdom of Kahlil Gibran
Will peace be on earth while the sons of misery are slaving in the fields
to feed the strong and fill the stomachs of the tyrants?
Will ever peace come and save them from the clutches of destitution?

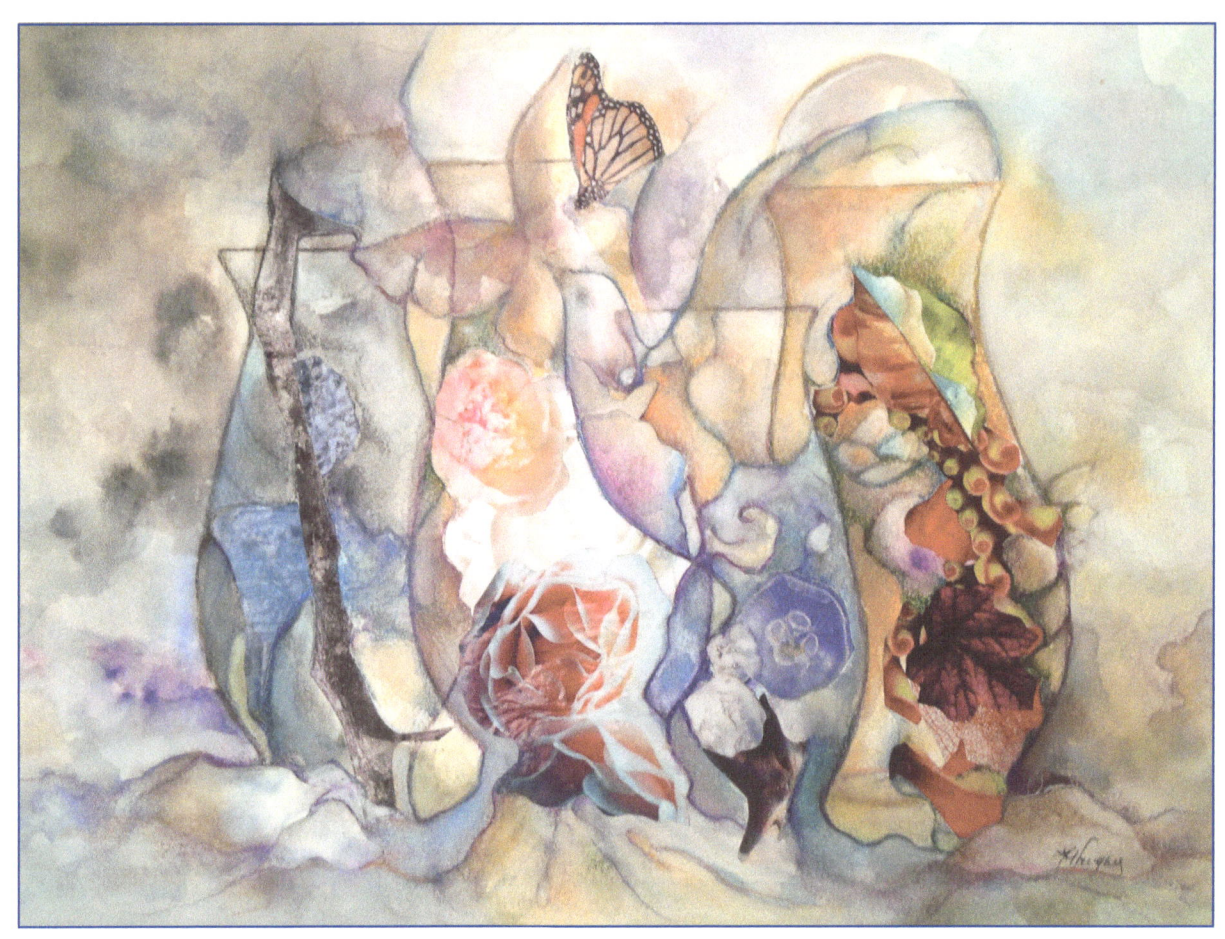

Seasonal Mosaic

The Seasons have their own distinct personalities
and stay within the certain limitations of who they are,
yet they flow and blend together seamlessly.

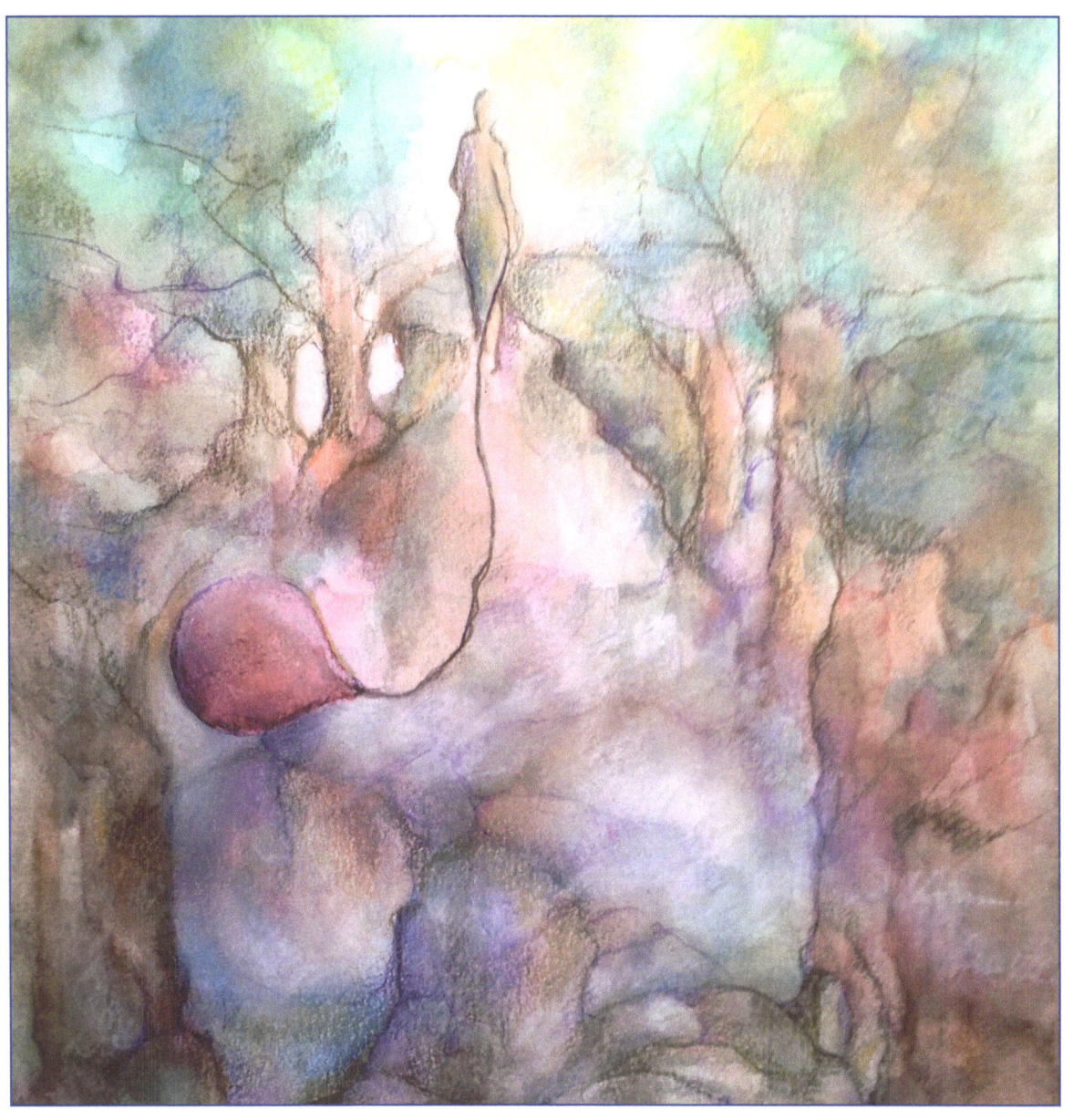

A Path Less Traveled

I have never followed the crowd and have made a path where there was none.
Through the thicket, and without a map, I have pursued my own identity.
The balloon? Enjoying the journey, one day at a time.

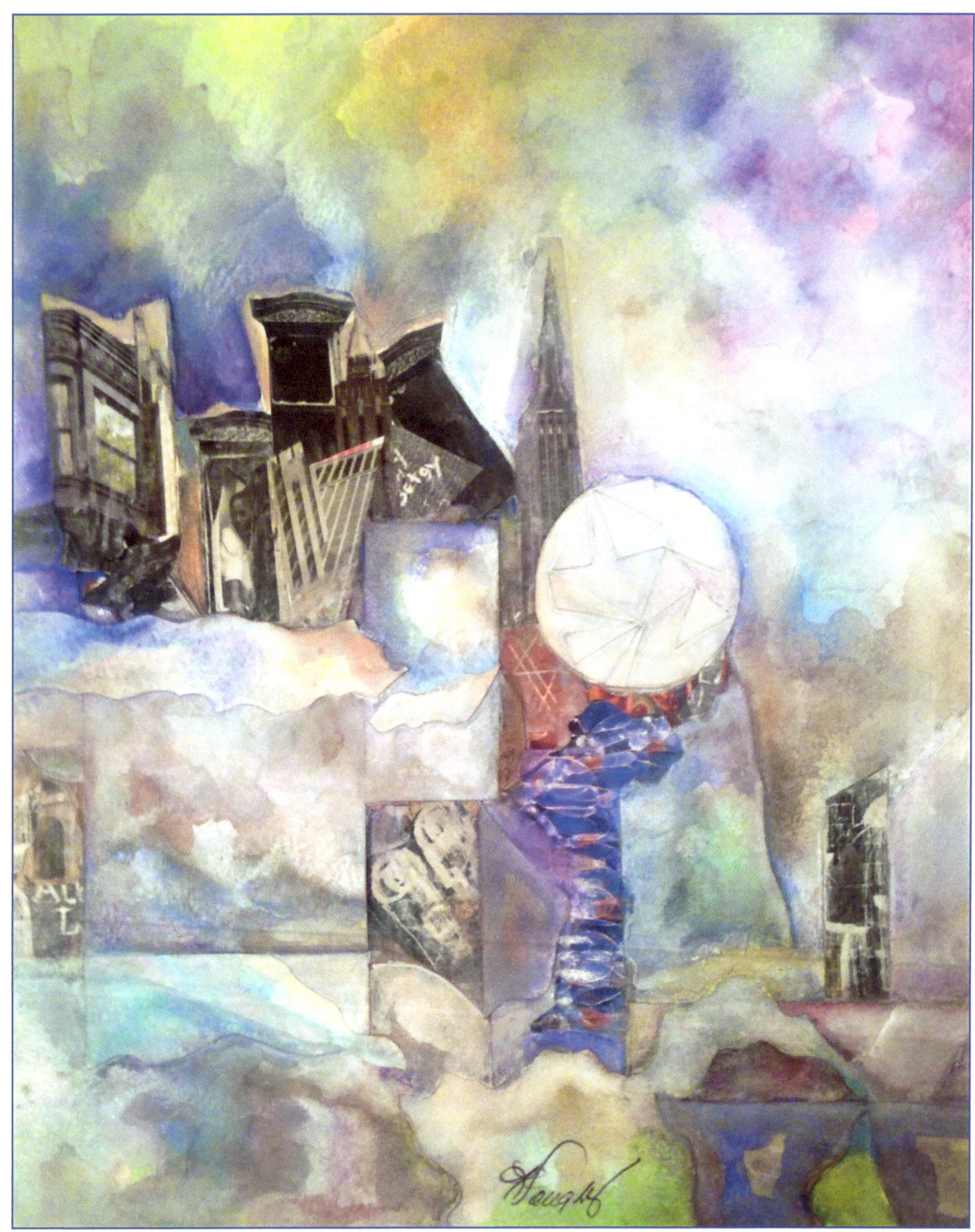

City of Hope

I painted this piece contemplating diversity and division between
the seemingly comfortable population, in contrast to the strife
and struggle of living among the common.
—Karen Haughey

Were poverty and sorrow abolished,
the spirit of man would be like an empty tablet
with nothing inscribed save the signs of selfishness and greed.
—Kahlil Gibran

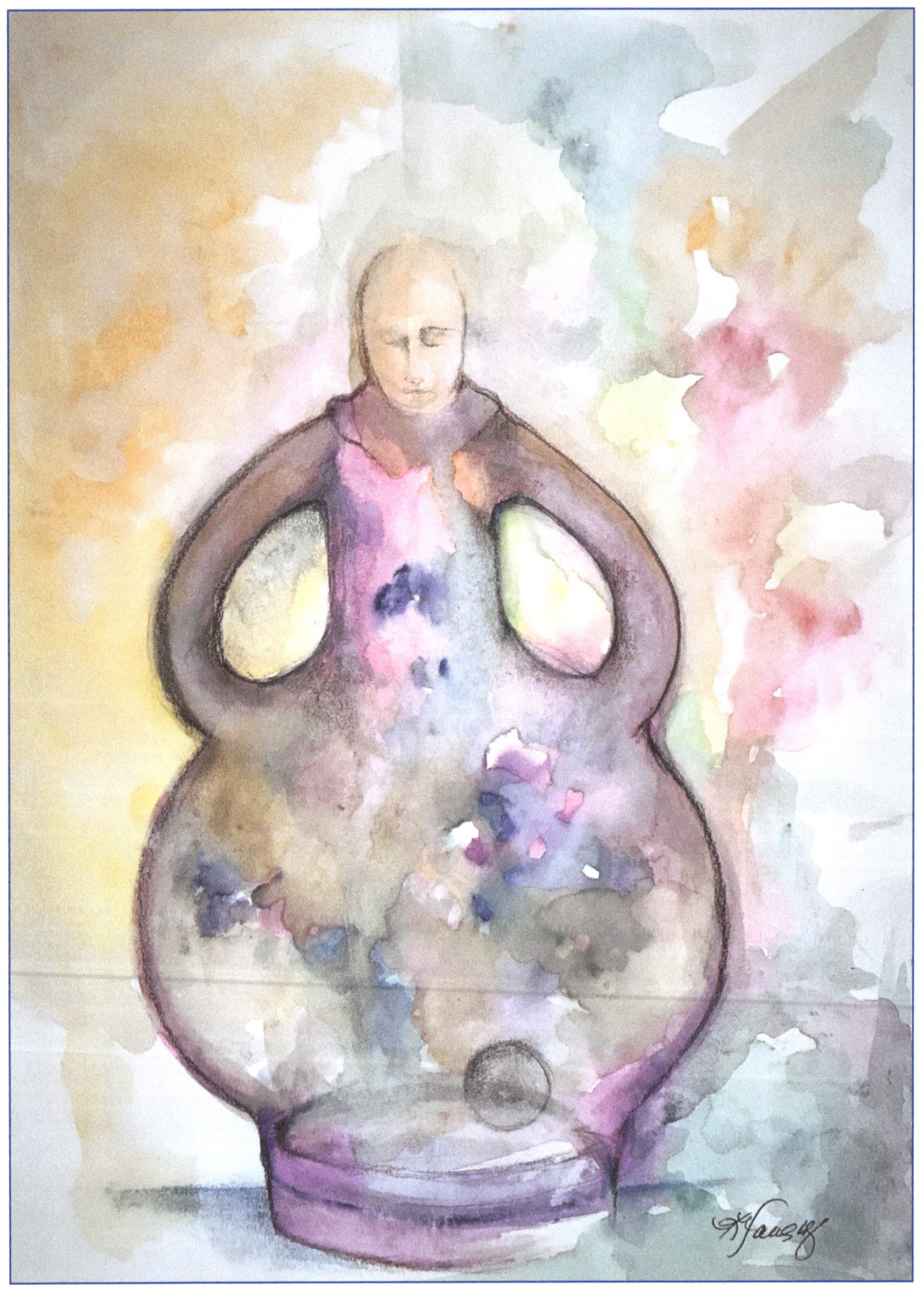

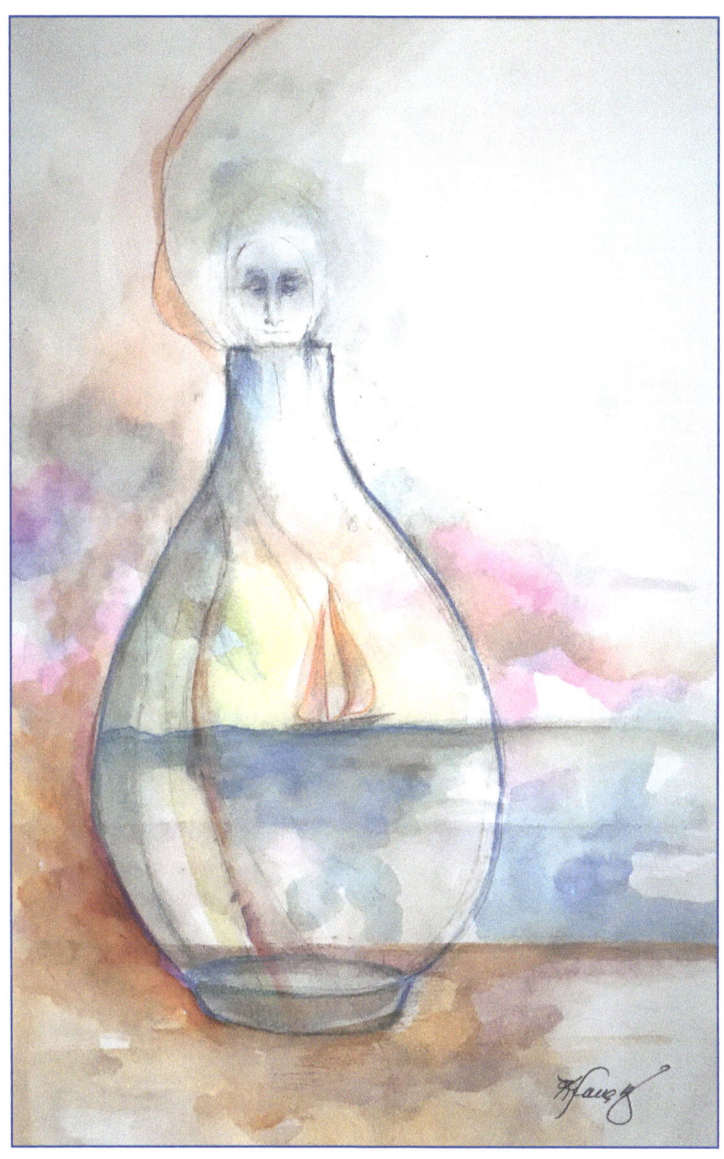

VESSEL *(left page)*
SAILING VESSEL *(right page)*

We are all vessels, carrying within us personal thoughts, spiritual values, creativity, distinct separate journeys and paths that no one else can share.

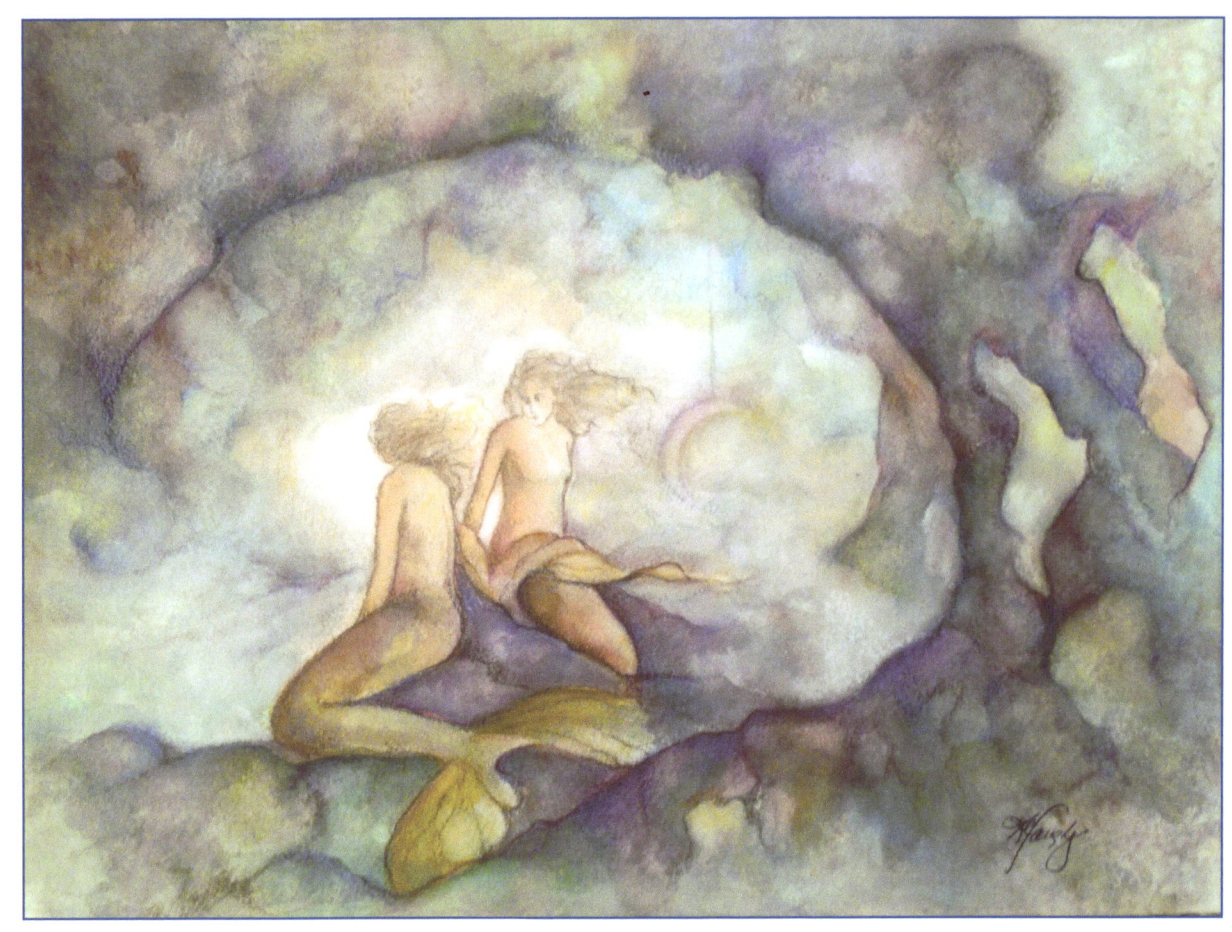

HIGH TIDE
(Left Page)

Deep within underwater caverns are mermaids
conversing with the evening moon, stars and clouds
that keep their heartfelt secrets safe.

WONDERMENT
(Right Page)

Seeking and discovering over a lifetime,
where all is wonder, mystery and adventure.
Close your eyes, and imagine your life as a mermaid.

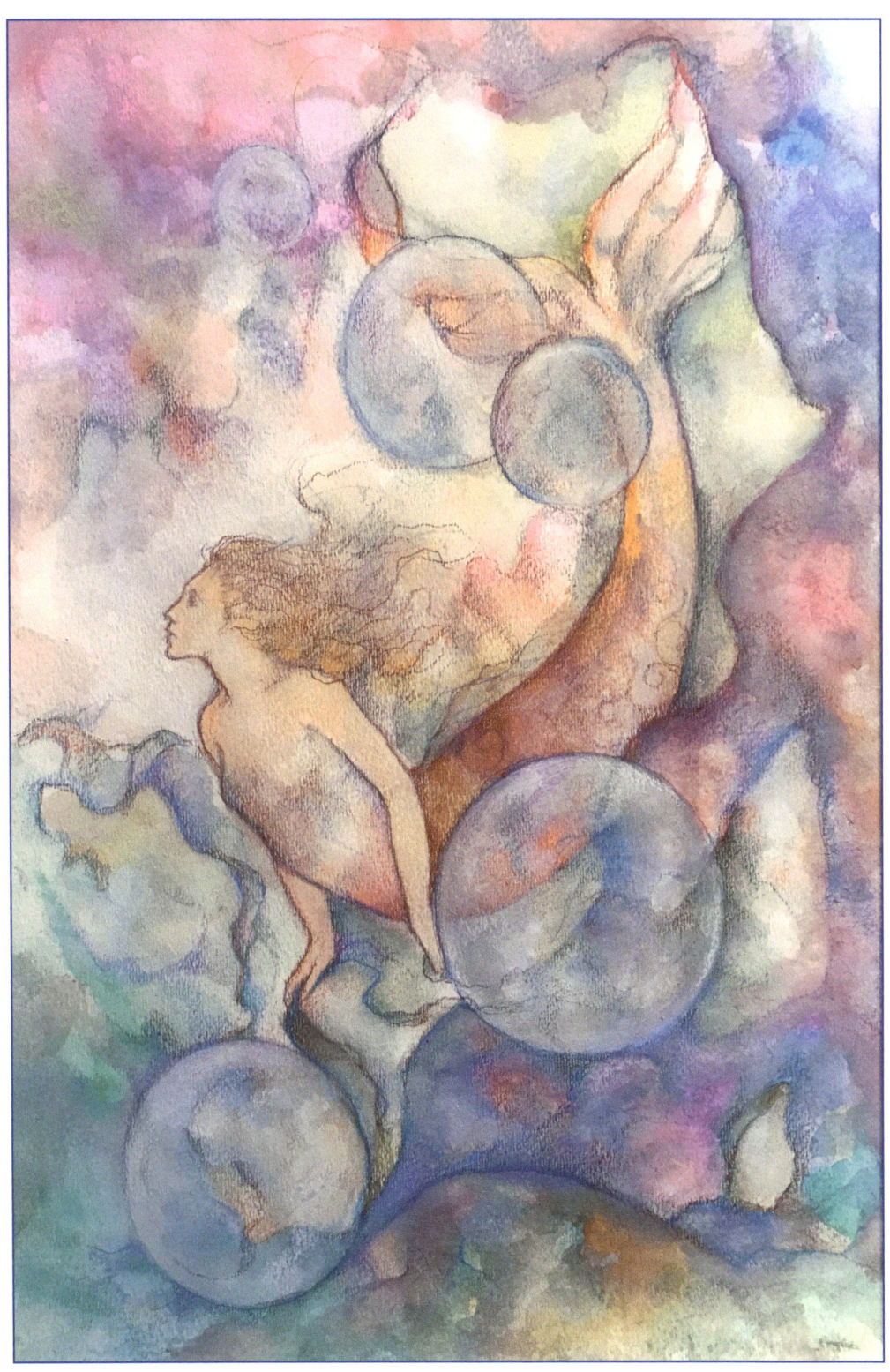

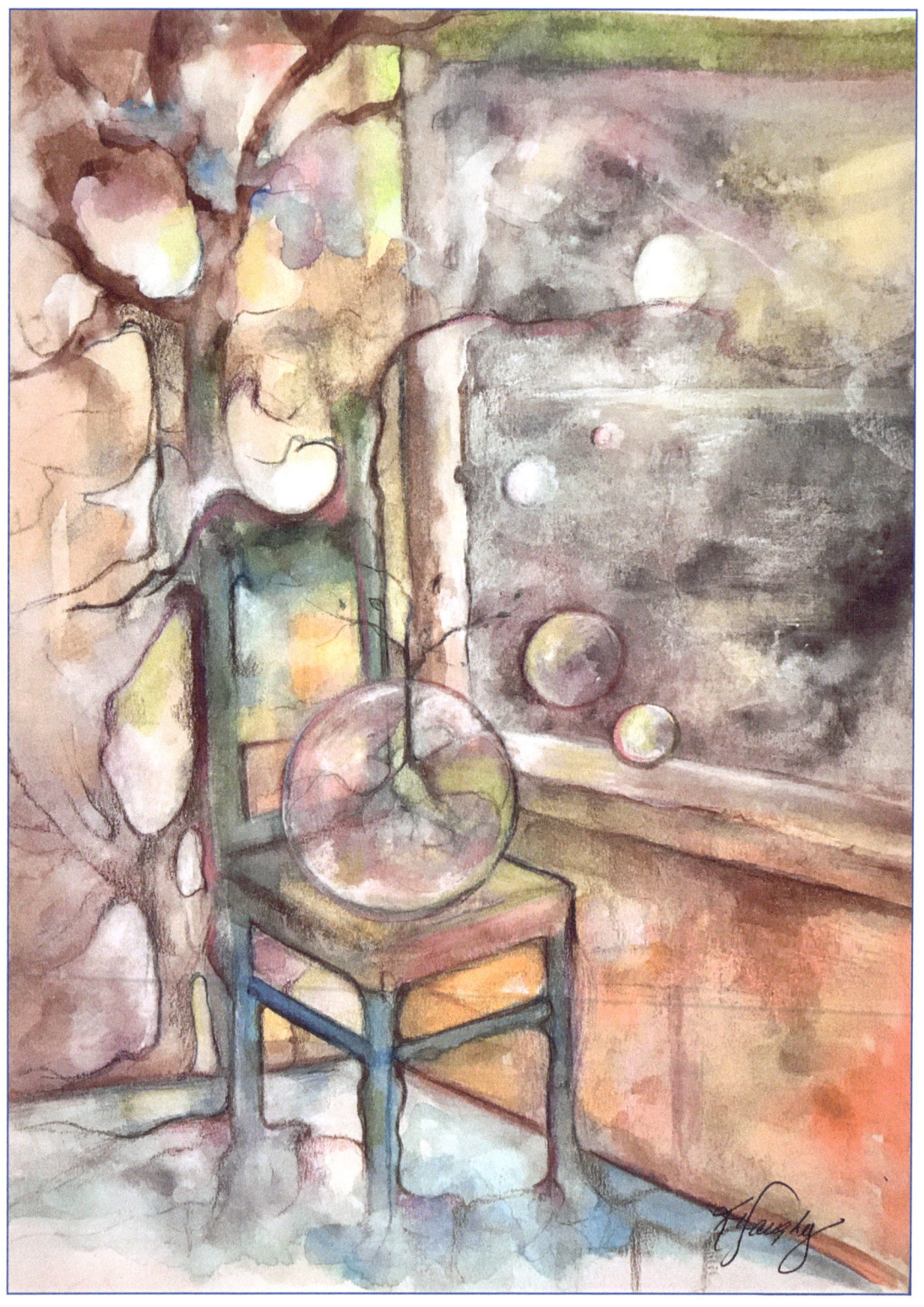

The Wishing Chair

As I sit contemplating the night sky I cast forth wishes in hope for peace.
I have planted seeds and declared intentions for manifestation in all that is good.
As in prayer, believe with expectancy.

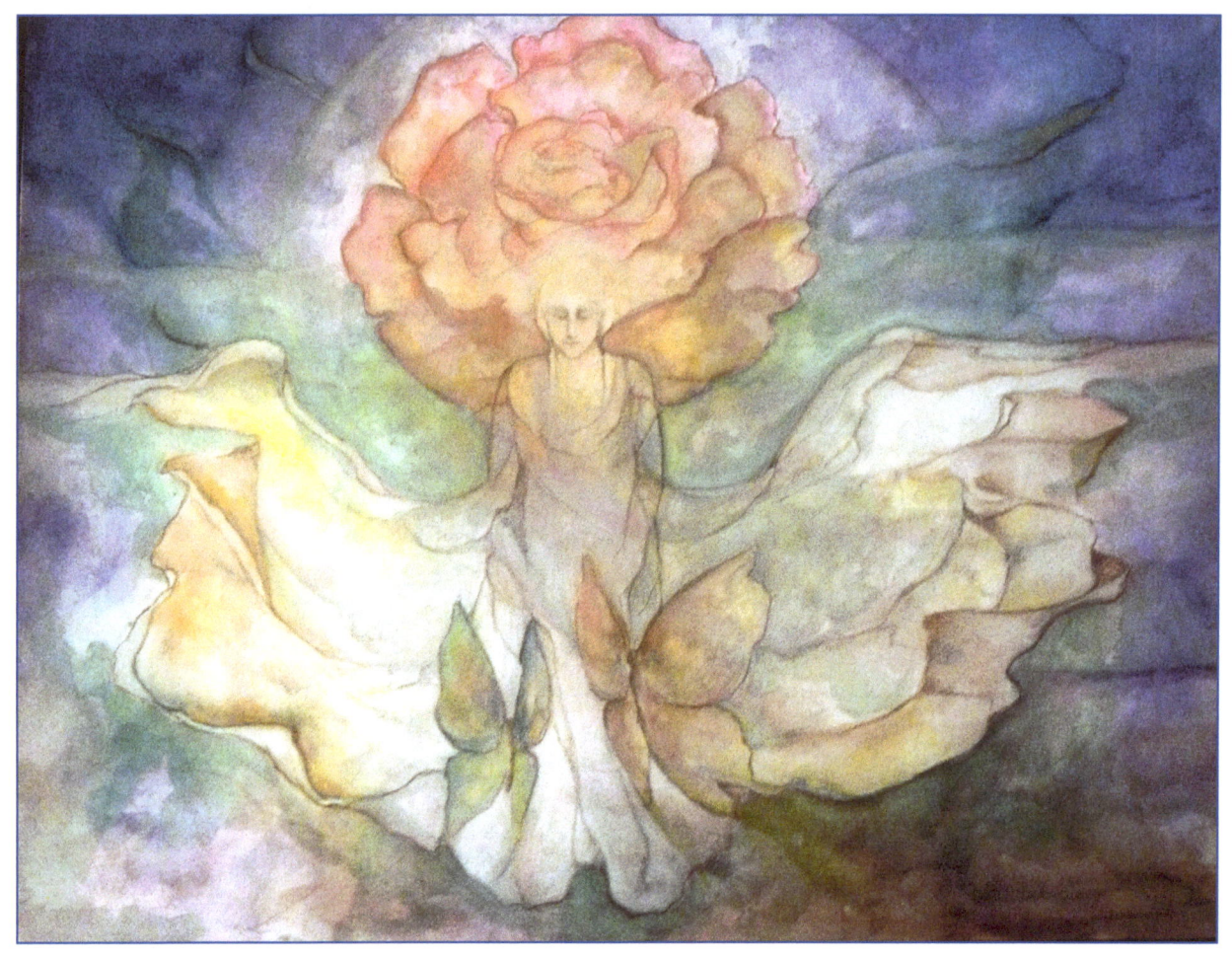

NATURE

Veiled in silence, nature will unfold her glory and beauty,
yet also extend her wrath. We cannot bend the will of nature,
but we can seek her among the flora, flowing water,
majestic mountains, trees, rainbows, rain,
lightening, thunder, and by the breath of life itself.

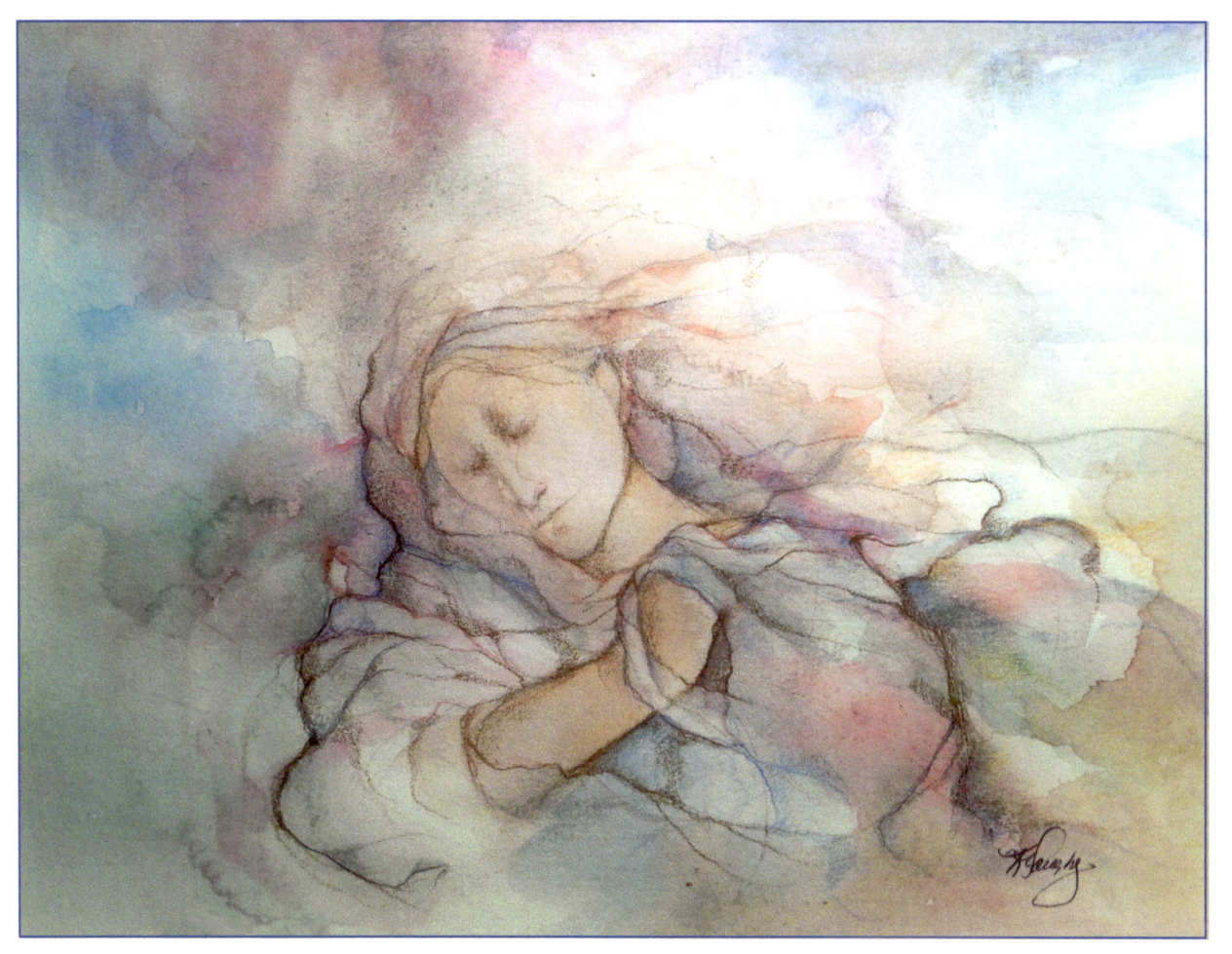

Repose

Looking within the depths of my soul,
I find peace, comfort, rest and renewal.

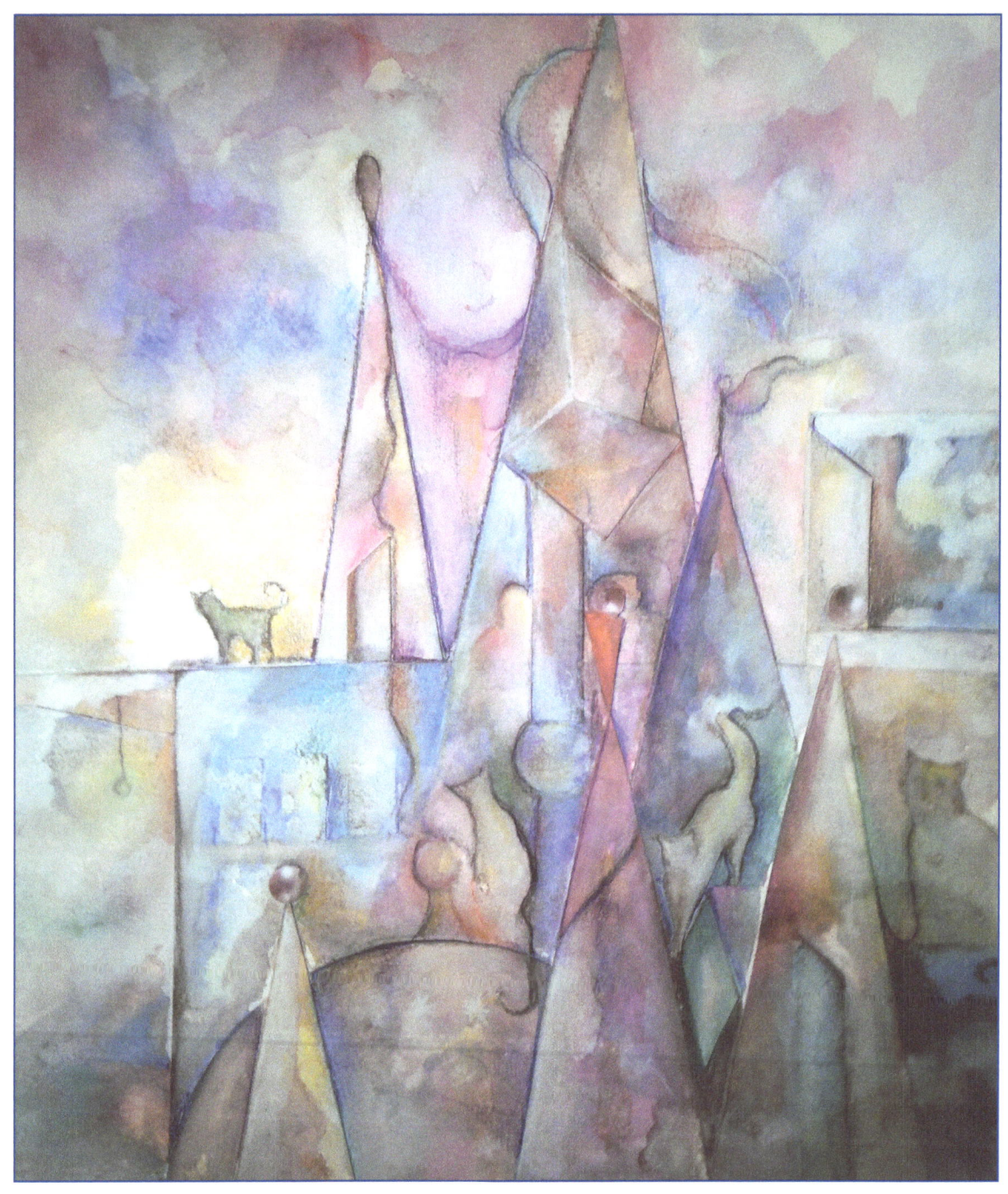

CAT TALES

Being an avid cat lover, I imagined and created spirals and towers
where felines can play and explore without limitation.

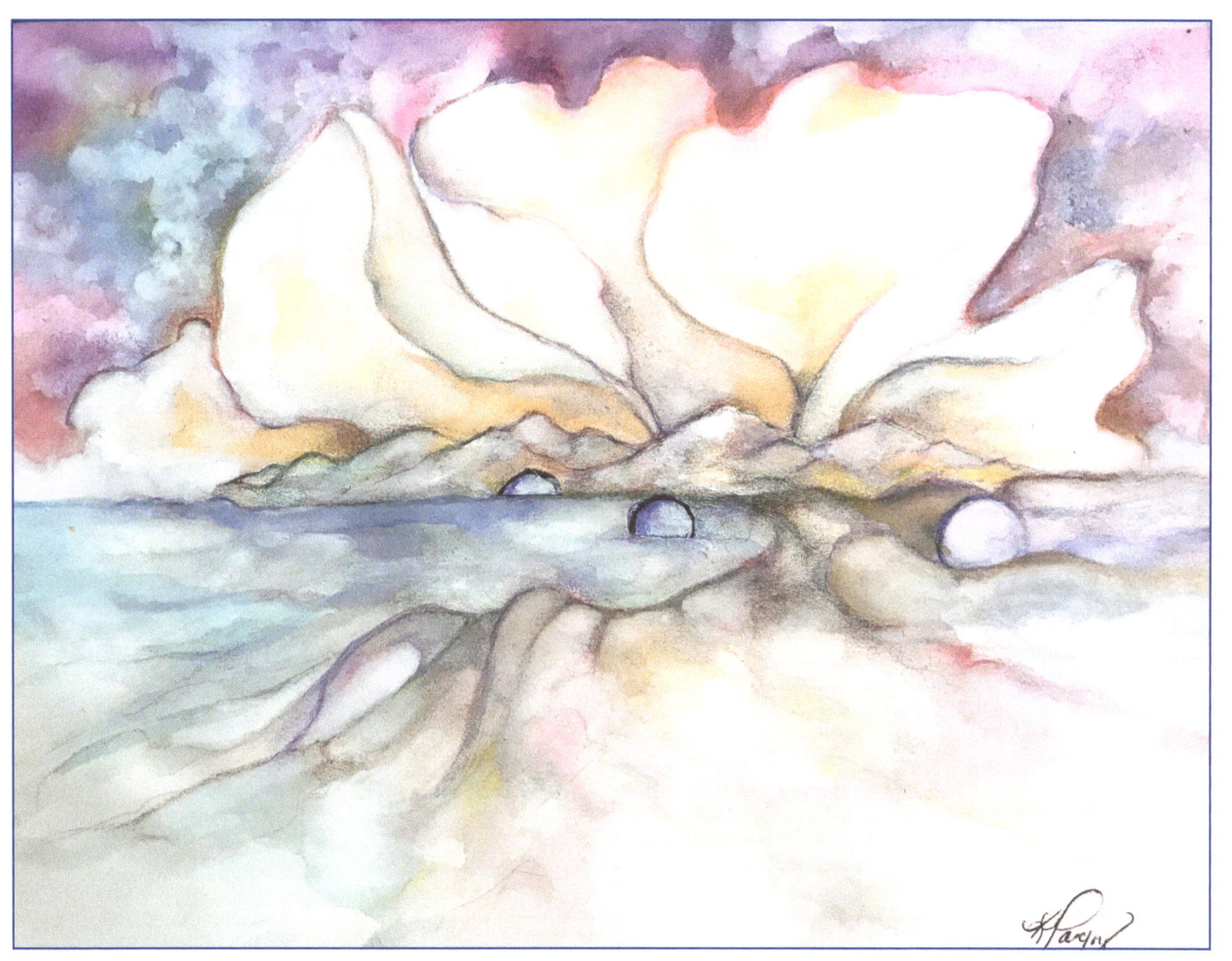

MINDSCAPE

In the creativity of my mind, I travel to places unknown to others.
Visions manifesting into landscapes, and beings that
I have not seen before, manifesting from brush to paper.

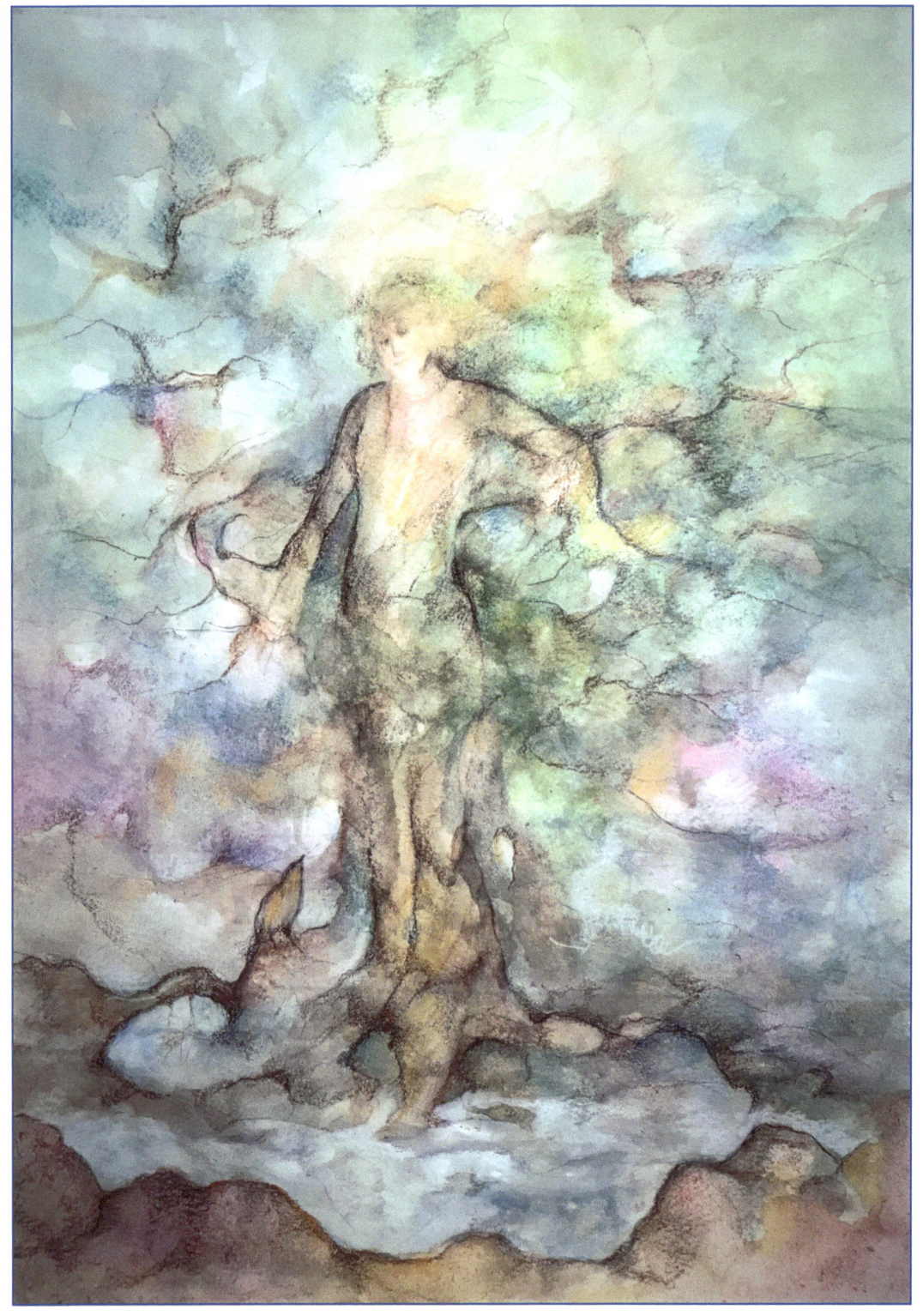

Morning Conversation

What do we know of the secrecy in nature?
Imagine the languages and conversations spoken
among its many creatures, trees and flora
that mortals do not understand.

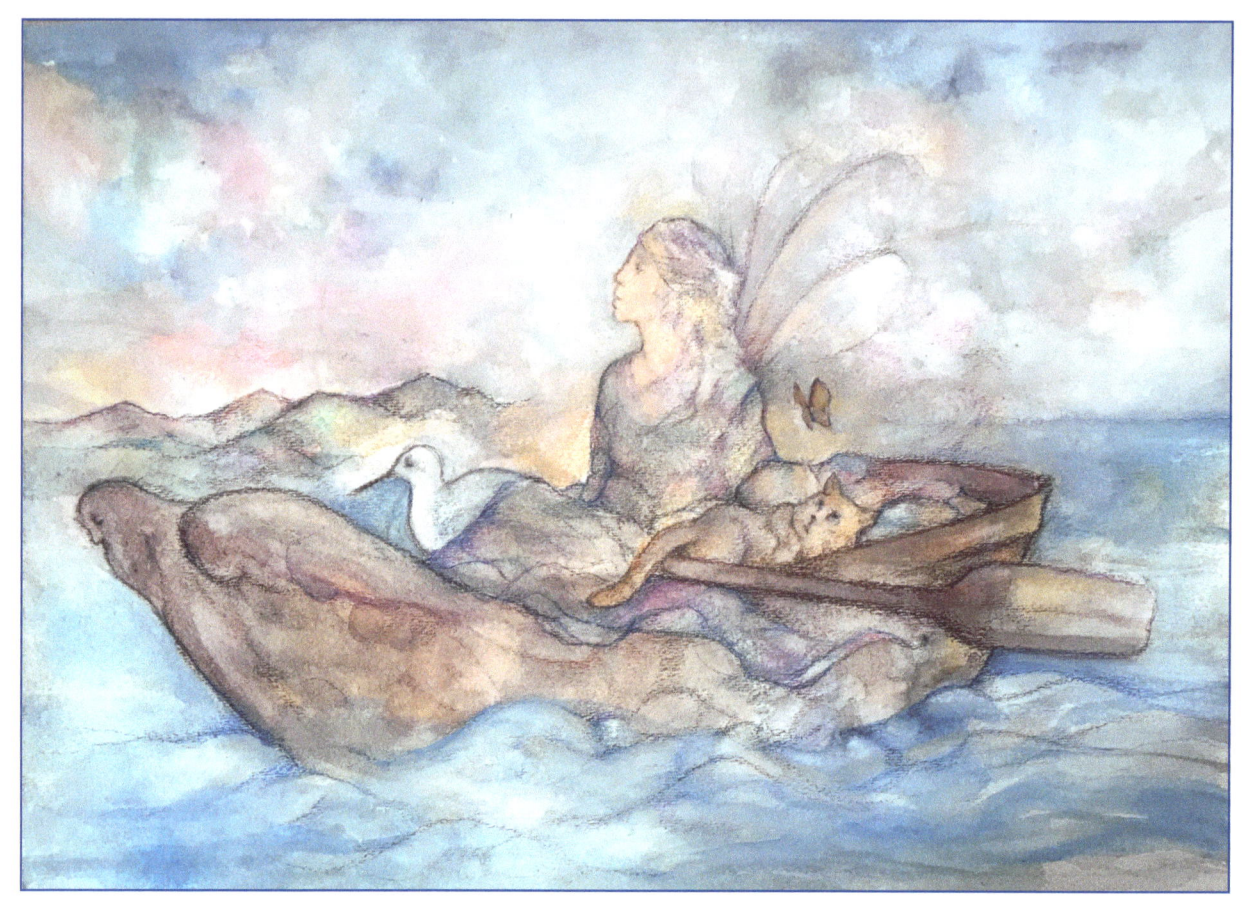

Peaceful Voyage

An unwritten fairytale of friends and fairies
that exist in the mind of children, or anyone
willing to embrace the tranquil land and sea
residing within the realms
of our playful imaginations.

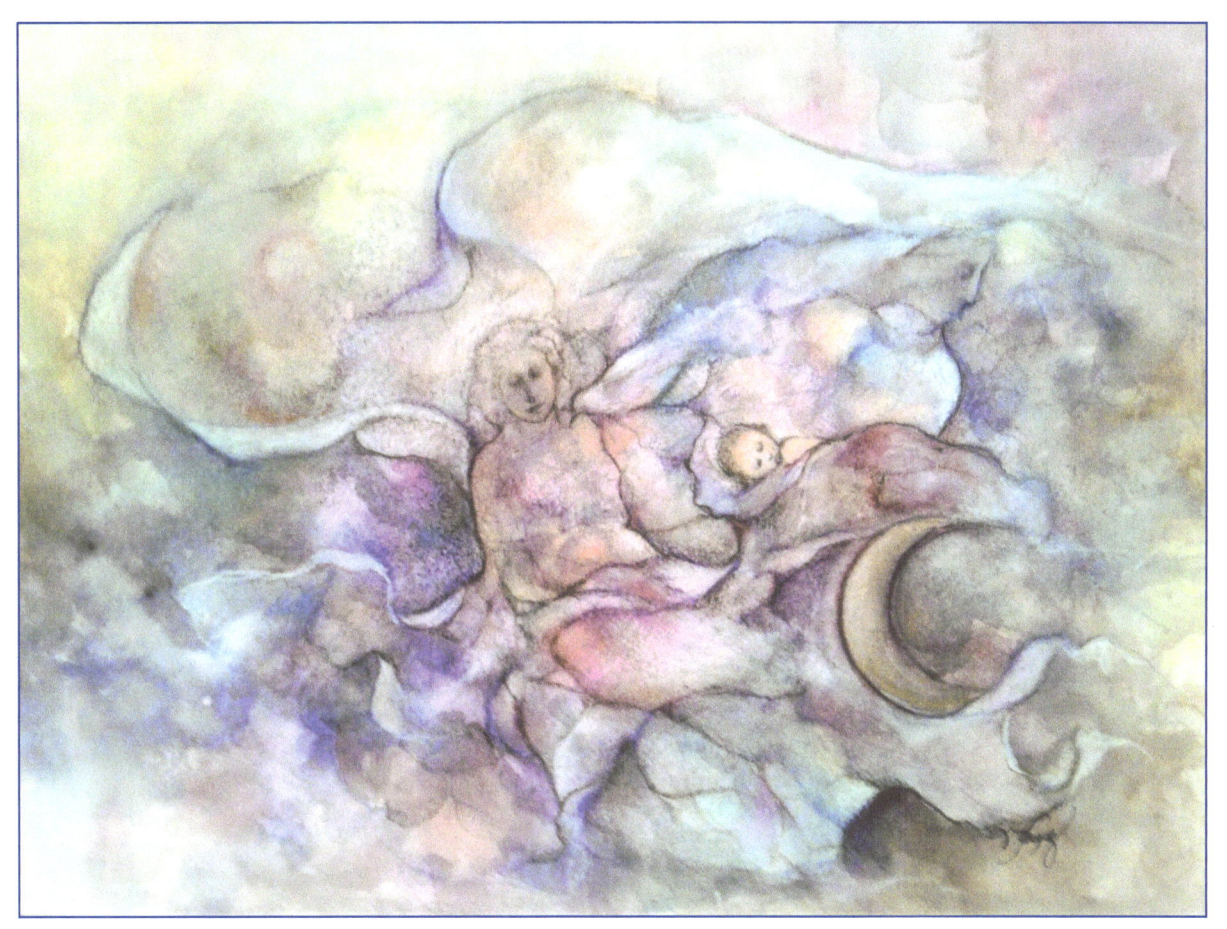

Slumber

Within the safe and sacred arms of sleep,
may we find renewal, peace and hope for a new day.

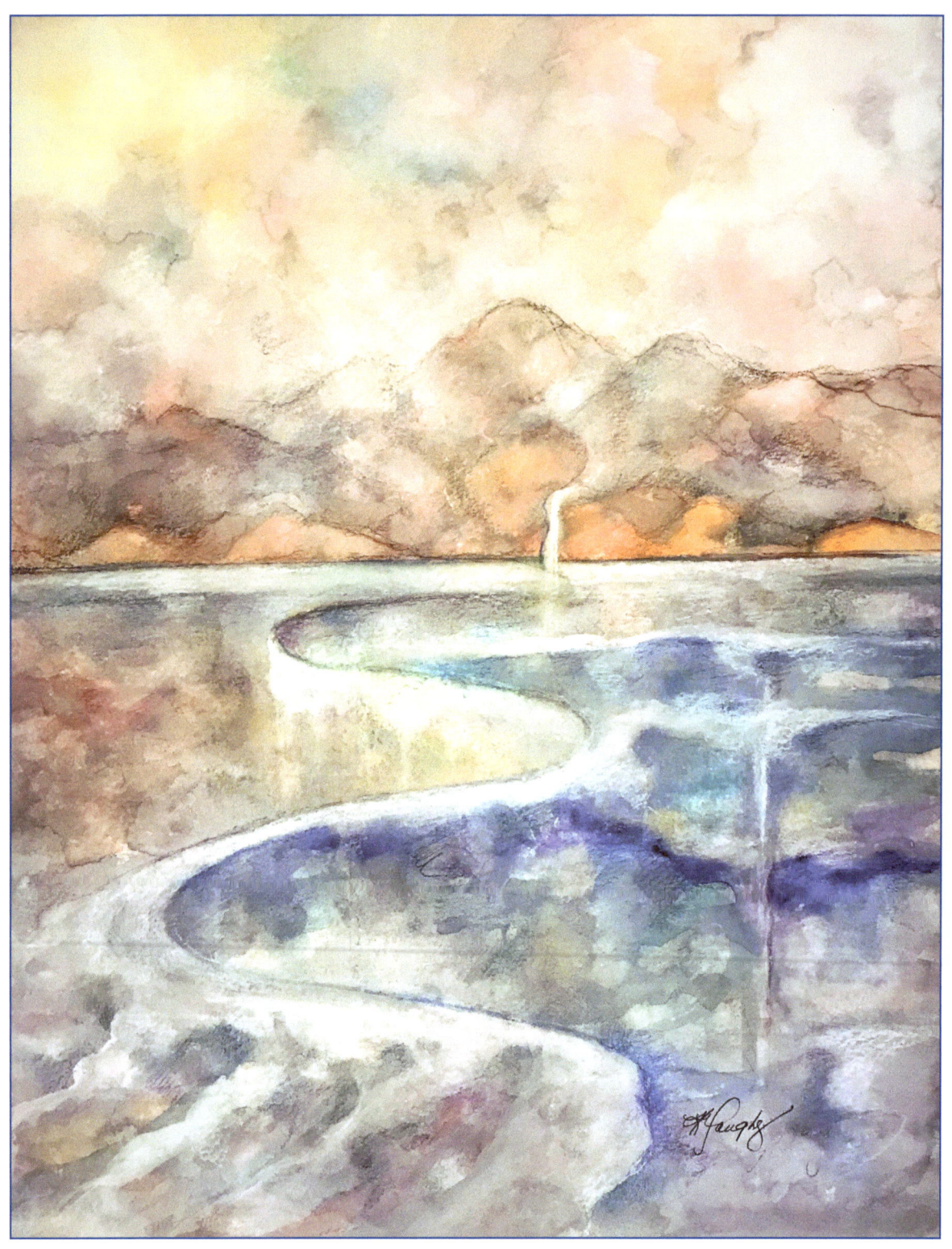

Hidden Cove

This painting had elements of continual change,
and ended up as a mysterious landscape.
Months later, after I completed the painting,
I happened upon a photograph
of Death Valley National Park,
located in the Southern part of California.
Although I have never been there,
one of the geographic photographs
was very similar to the landscape I painted.
I researched the photographer,
as I felt compelled to share it,
in return, he sent me a visual reference
of the actual location I had painted.

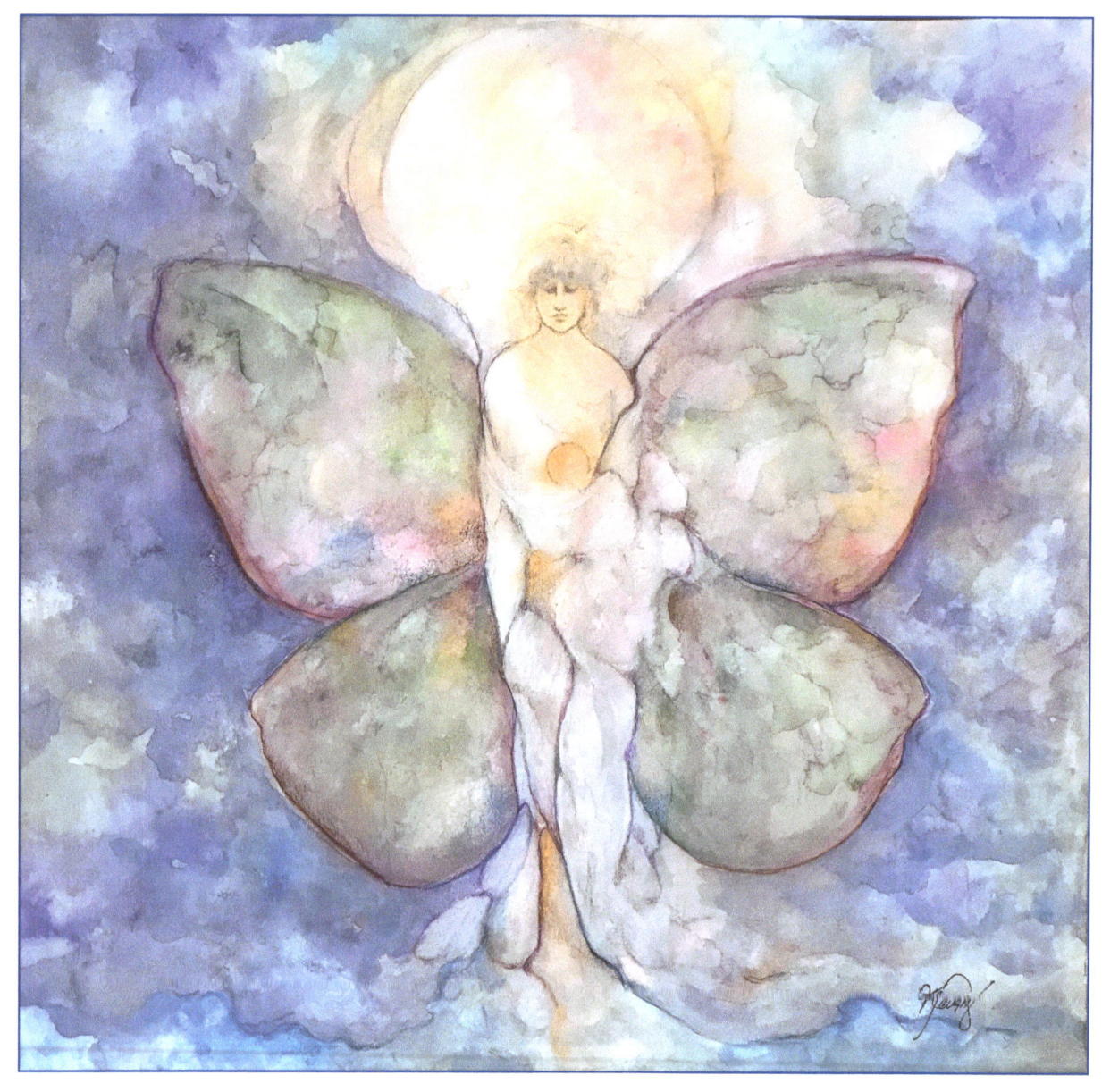

Cocoon

Rebirth and transformation.
From earthbound to the expansion of unfolded wings.
Flight, freedom.

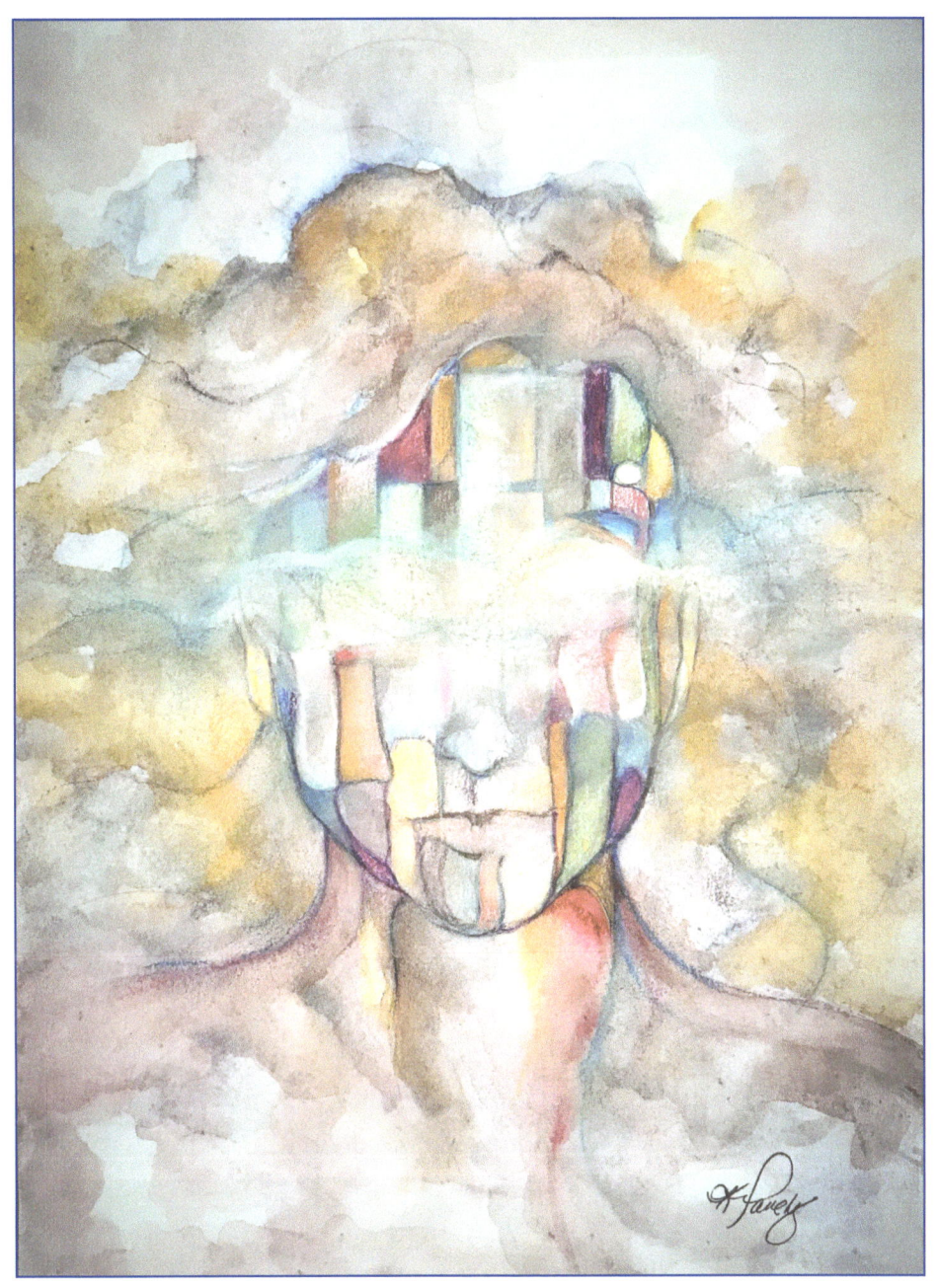

WINDOWS OF THE MIND

My mind feels like a library of information,
unwritten manuscripts, and unexplained forms of thought.
Creativity manifesting into visual reality.

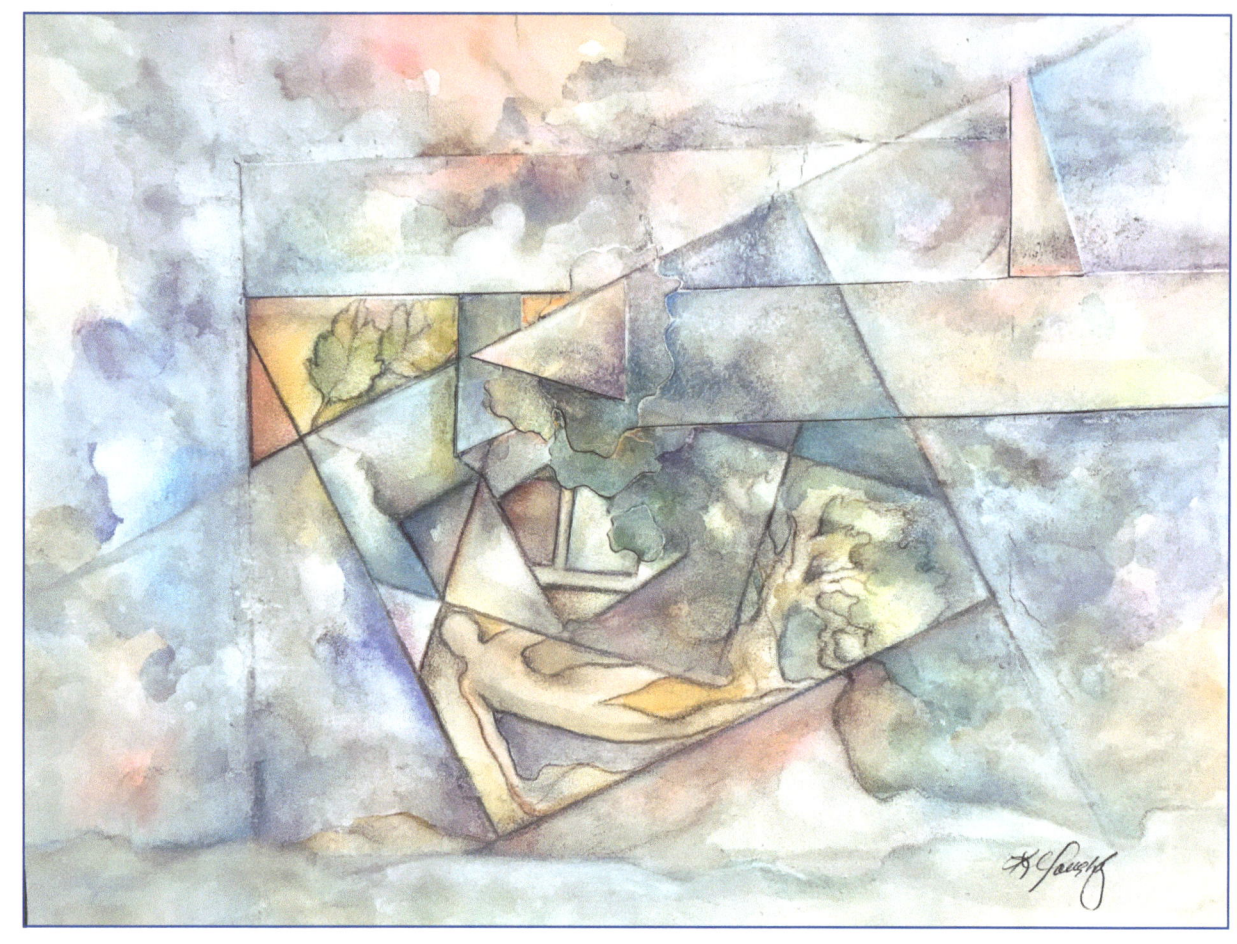

Prism

(left Page)

Like a vast kaleidoscope of color that encompasses the seasons,
people, creativity, and all of nature, it continually blends itself
and all elements into boundless wonder and potential.

Blessing Tree

(right Page)

To sit and meditate under the blessing tree you will also seek her comfort and peace.
Where birds build their nests, she also bears witness to the changing of seasons,
offering fruit and flowers as gifts from her willowy branches,
then changes the hue of leaves into gold during the fall, casting off her color
to the winter wind, and returning to shades of green in the warmth of the spring.

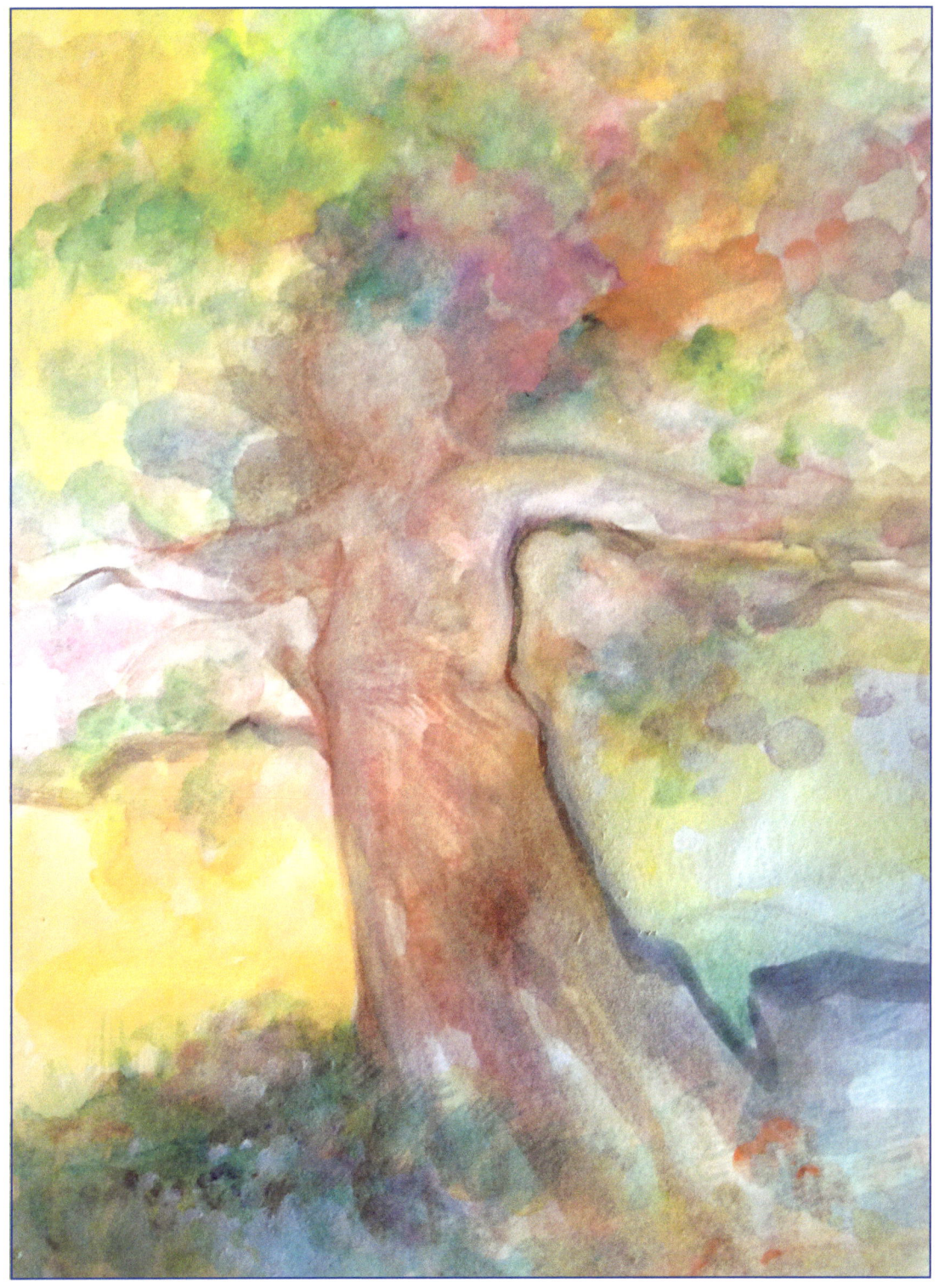

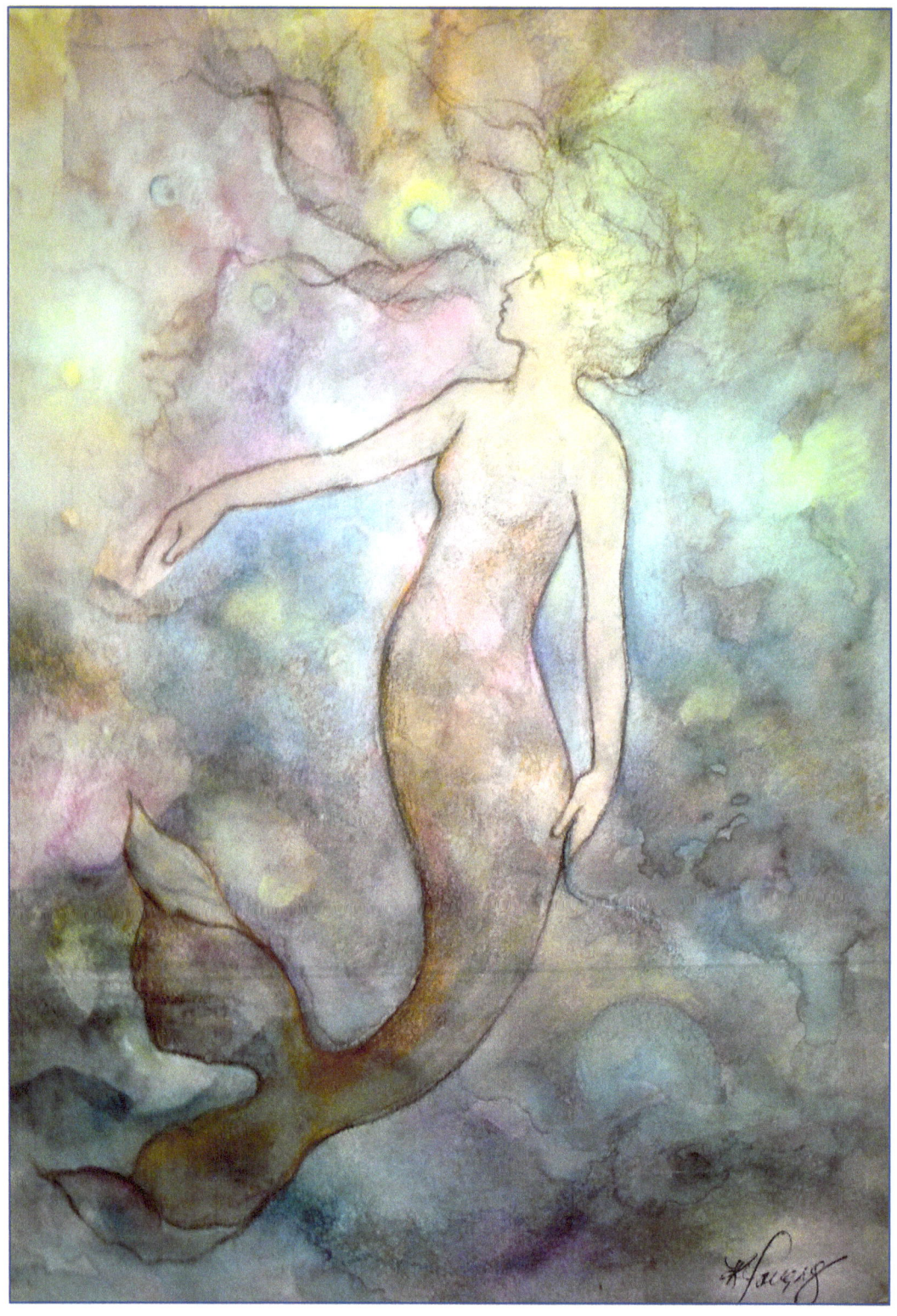

DRIFT

Mermaids, sea nymphs drifting under the ocean waves.
Peaceful abandonment of care and woe.
Do they choose to hide from the mortal world?

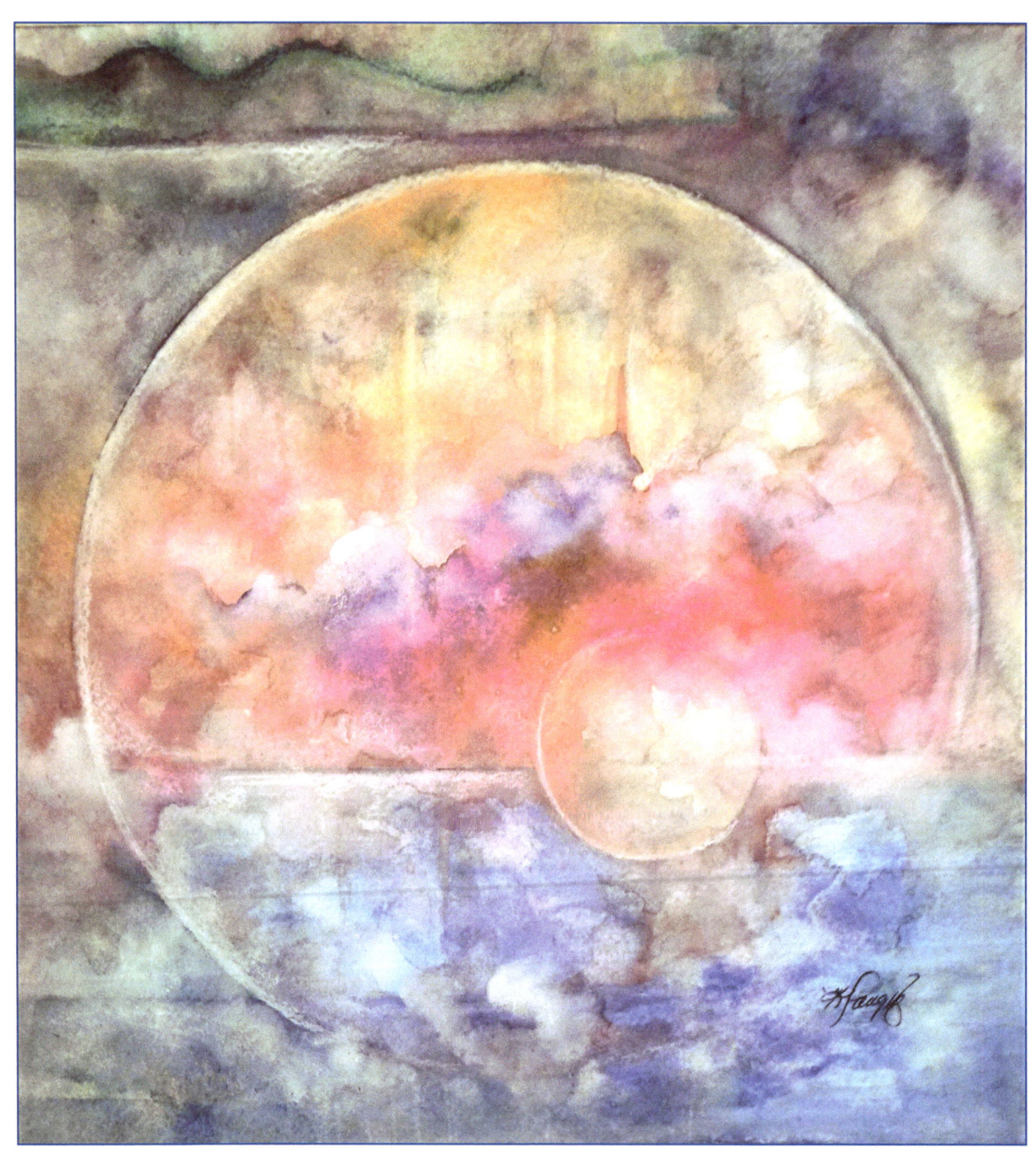

Profusion Mandala

Circles, color, and the continuation of life in all of its form.
Day into night, season into season, death and rebirth.
Mandalas are the creative purpose of giving expression
and form into something that does not exist.
The process is that of the ascending spiral, growing
upward while returning again to the same point.

Jungian Analyst,
—Marie Louise van Franz

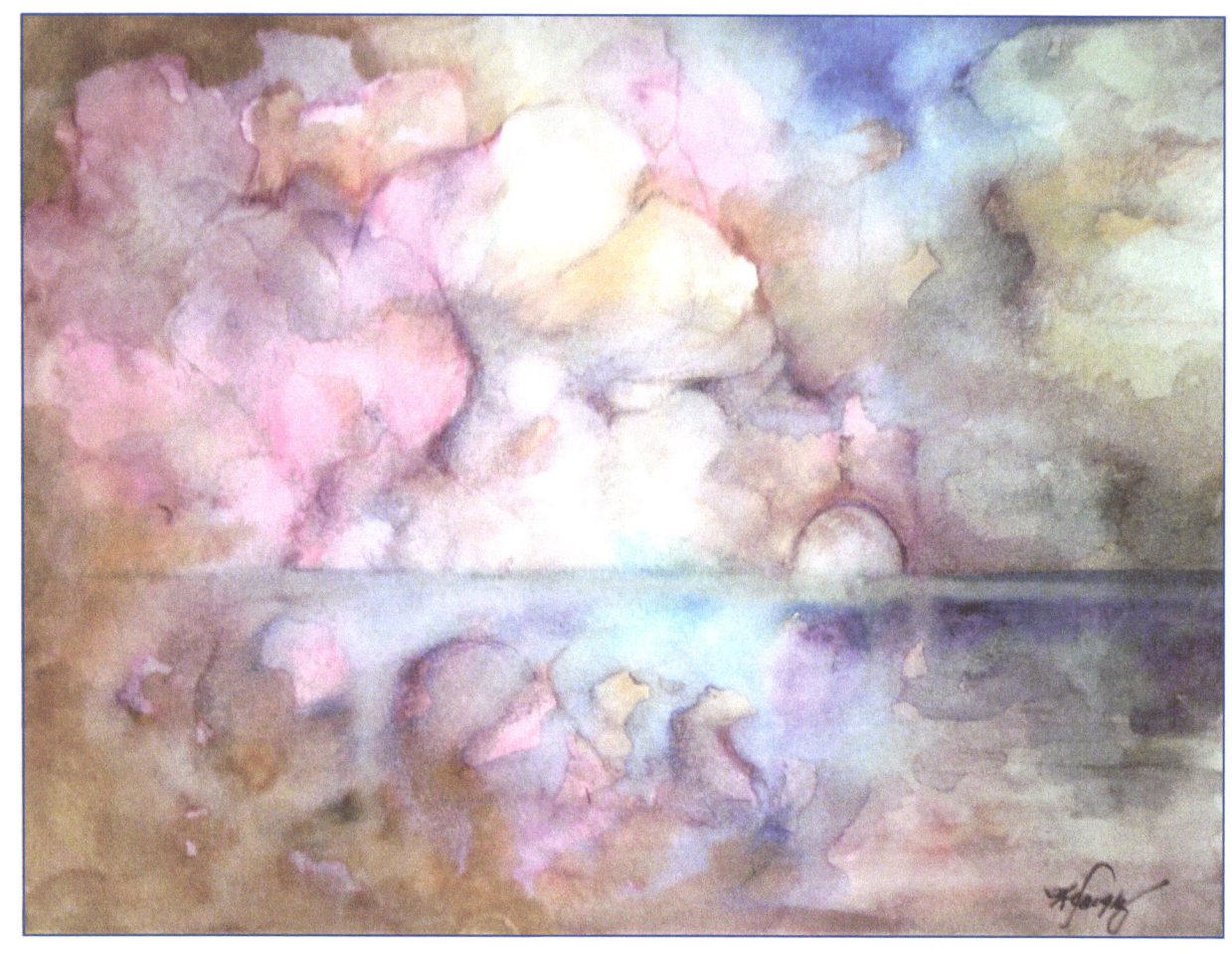

Sunset

Billowy clouds of color returning
the light of the sun back to the sea's horizon,
is where I send thoughts of thankfulness at the end of the day.

About the Author

I have been a professional artist for over forty years, and developed a style which is a combination of watercolor, pastel and gouache.

I have been creating ethereal subject matter since 1984. Each painting begins with an inner vision or concept, and then my creative muses bring each piece to final conclusion.

Published Books 1995 – 1998

Angels, Guardians of the Light – Hay House, Carlsbad, California
Gratitude, Hay House – Carlsbad, California
One Source Sacred Journeys – Markowitz Publications, Honolulu, Hi.
The Angels Talk – Penguin Putman, N.Y., N.Y.
Angel Answers – Simon Schuster, N.Y., N.Y.

Television and Radio Broadcasts 1987 – 2003

Explorations of the Mind, Fremont, Newark, Ca. Producer / Host / Public broadcast television.
Dateline NBC, New York, N.Y. Televised public broadcast interview.
Creative Encounters, San Jose, Ca. Televised public broadcast interview
The Gabrielle Show, Los Angeles, Ca. Televised public broadcast interview.

Selected Published Art and Articles 1987 – present

Penguin Books, N.Y., N.Y. *Angel Answers*, cover design, author, Andrew Ramer,
Angel Times Magazine, National Magazine Articles.
San Jose Mercury News, San Jose, Ca., *Argus Newspaper*, Fremont, Ca. Personal Interviews.
Master Your Mind Audio Cassette Covers/ Designs.
Spirit Art Greeting Card Co., Minneapolis, Minnesota, Greeting cards.
1996 Designer's Showcase, San Jose, Ca. Artist presentation
Fresh Start Surgical Team, San Diego, Ca. Artist presentation
Hay House, San Diego, Ca., *Angels, Guardians of the Light*. International book publication.
Realizing Potentials Publications, New Mexico, *Angelic Awakenings*, author, Jessica Eccles,
Book cover design.
World Disc Productions, San Juan Island, Washington. Peter Sterling's C.D Covers.
Dream, Electric Angels, Fremont, Ca., C.D. Cover Designs.
ARC, San Diego, Ca., Book Cover and Material Designs.
Connections Puzzles, Honolulu, Hi. Art / Designs for puzzles.
Tri City Voice newspaper, Fremont, Ca. Interview

www.ingramcontent.com/pod-product-compliance
Lightning Source LLC
Chambersburg PA
CBHW040414220526
45473CB00004B/1239